Show What You Know® on the 7th Grade FCAT

Student Workbook

Show What You Know® Publishing
Columbus, OH U.S.A.

Published by:
Show What You Know® Publishing
P.O. Box 341348
Columbus, OH 43234-1348
Phone: 614-764-1211
www.showwhatyouknowpublishing.com
www.passthecat.com

Printed in the United States of America
05 04 03 02   20 19 18 17 16 15 14 13 12 11 10 9 8 7 6 5 4 3 2 1

ISBN: 1-884183-90-5

About the Contributors

The content of this book was written BY teachers FOR teachers and students and was designed specifically for the 7th-Grade Florida Comprehensive Assessment Test (FCAT). Contributions to the Reading and Mathematics sections of this book were also made by the educational publishing staff at Show What You Know® Publishing. Dr. Jolie S. Brams, a clinical child and family psychologist, is the contributing author of the Test-Taking Strategies and Test Anxiety chapters of this book. Without the contributions of these people, this book would not be possible.

Acknowledgements

Show What You Know® Publishing acknowledges the following for their efforts in making this assessment material available for Florida students, parents, and teachers:

Cindi Englefield, President/Publisher
Eloise Boehm-Sasala, Vice President/Managing Editor
Mercedes Baltzell, Production Editor
Scott D. Stuckey, Editor
Lainie Burke, Desktop Publisher/Assistant Editor
Jennifer Harney, Illustrator/Cover Designer
Kathie Christian, Proofreader
Erica T. Klingerman, Proofreader

Table of Contents

Introduction

Show What You Know® on the 7th-Grade FCAT is designed to help you familiarize yourself with the seventh-grade Florida Comprehensive Assessment Test (FCAT).

The Test Anxiety and Test-Taking Strategies chapters were written especially for seventh-grade students. These sections offer tips such as how to take tests and how to avoid test stress.

Chapters on Reading and Mathematics cover each Benchmark assessed by the 7th-Grade FCAT. Sample questions are given for each individual Benchmark to help you learn how each type of question may be asked. Additional 40-question practice tests are also included for Reading and Mathematics. These tests will help you become familiar with the types of questions you will be asked on the FCAT. Each test is a great opportunity for you to practice your test-taking skills.

Types of Questions

Multiple-Choice Questions

On the 7th-Grade FCAT, you will select from four possible answer choices and fill in a bubble in your answer book. Although multiple-choice items sometimes ask for the recall of facts, most of the sample items demand a more complex thought process. Each multiple-choice item on the assessment is scored 0 (incorrect) or 1 (correct). Each correct answer adds one point to the total assessment score.

Gridded-Response Questions

On the Mathematics section of the FCAT, you will also be asked to answer gridded-response questions. Each question requires a numerical answer, which should be filled into a bubble grid. The bubble grid consists of 5 columns. Each column contains the numbers 0-9 and a decimal point; the middle three columns contain a fraction bar as well. You do not need to include any commas for numbers greater than 999. When filling in your answer, only fill in one bubble per column. All gridded-response questions are constructed so the answer will fit into the grid. You can start your answer in any column, as long as when you continue to the right, your response fits in the grid. Be sure to write your answer in the grid above the bubbles as well, in case clarification is needed. Answers can be given in whole number, fraction, or decimal form. For questions involving measurements, the unit of measure required for the answer will be provided for you. You will also be instructed when to round your answer in a particular way. Some example responses are given below.

Answer: 23,901

Answer: 26.5

Answer: 0.071

Answer: $\frac{3}{8}$

Test Anxiety

What is Test Anxiety?

"Test anxiety" is just a fancy name for "feeling nervous about tests." Everyone knows what it is like to feel nervous. Feeling nervous is not a good feeling! Most important, when we are nervous, it gets in the way of doing our best on tests.

Students who have test anxiety do not make good decisions on tests. They cannot pay attention to the test, plan out their answers, or remember what they know. They stare at the paper and no answer is there! They become "stuck" and cannot move on. Because their minds are running in a hundred different directions, they forget to do simple things such as read directions or fill in an answer bubble correctly. The more anxious they become, the "dumber" they feel. Even though they are not dumb, their anxiety makes them feel terrible about themselves. The worse they feel, the less confident they feel, and the more poorly they do on tests. That is why it is important to get test anxiety under control. After all, the whole idea of the FCAT is to show all that you know!

It doesn't really matter whether you talk about being stressed, worried, nervous, or anxious. It all adds up to the same problem! Luckily, there is much we can do to feel calmer and more sure of ourselves when taking tests.

Do Other Seventh Graders Have Test Anxiety?

You bet! If you care about school at all, you probably are going to have some anxiety or worry about tests. If you are a test worrier, either once in a while or all the time, don't let it worry you! Most likely, many of your classmates and friends also have fearful feelings about tests. Even your parents and teachers have had their own troubles with anxiety about taking tests or other challenges in their lives. Remember, you are not alone!

Unfortunately, few seventh-grade students like to talk about what bothers them. Sure, they might complain about many things, but not too many seventh graders want to say, "Hey! I'm really scared about that test next week." Everyone wants to seem "cool" and "grown up." Not talking to others about worries and anxiety only makes the situation worse. It makes us feel alone and makes us wonder if there is something "wrong" with us. Be brave! When you talk to your friends and teachers, you will find that they understand. They also can help you in many ways. You will feel much better for sharing your thoughts and feelings.

What Does it Feel Like to Have Test Anxiety?

Students who have test anxiety don't always feel exactly the same way, but they always feel bad! Here are some ways that many students feel when they have test anxiety.

- **Students who have test anxiety often do not think good things about themselves.**
  If you don't feel good about yourself, how can you feel good about how you will do on a test? It just doesn't make sense that you will be a super test taker if you do not have confidence in your own abilities. Students with test anxiety are usually not very proud of themselves. In spite of all the good things they could think about themselves, they only think about what they can't do. The less they think about themselves, the more anxious they feel. If anxious students could say some good things about themselves, they might feel less worried!

- **Students who have test anxiety have poor thinking habits.**
  A habit is simply a way we do things over and over again until it becomes so much a part of us we don't think about it anymore. Some habits are good; some habits are bad. Pay attention to what you do the next time you put on your shoes. Did you put on the right shoe before the left shoe? If so, you probably do it every time. That is a habit. While it probably doesn't make much difference whether you put on your right shoe first or your left shoe first, your thinking habit are important. If you always think negatively about yourself and your school work, especially tests, then it is difficult to be successful. Your negative thinking gets in the way of solving problems, studying for tests, and having the confidence to do well. When you have negative-thinking habits, everything seems awful, and when you are convinced things won't go your way, not surprisingly, that is usually how things turn out! Changing the way you think can also change your life.

- **Students who have test anxiety may feel physically uncomfortable or even ill.**
  It is important to know your mind and your body are connected. When you are feeling stressed about a test, your body is also feeling stressed. When students have test anxiety, their thoughts might cause them to have different physical symptoms and feelings. Their hearts might beat fast, their stomachs might hurt, they might get headaches, or they might find their hands are sweaty. Some students become so ill from anxiety that they end up missing school, which only puts them further and further behind. This makes them even more anxious and worried! The more worried they get, the sicker they feel, and the more school they miss. This is not a good situation! If you feel ill from anxiety, it is time to talk to a parent or a teacher right away.

- **Students who have test anxiety want to escape.**
  Test anxiety is a terrible feeling. It is normal to want to get away or to escape from that feeling. Most people's first idea is to run away, especially from tests. Students may do this by refusing to go to school or by spending time in the nurse's station. This does not solve any problems. In fact, it makes everything worse because the more you run away from problems, the less chance you have to solve those problems. When you try to escape, the problems are still there, but you have not worked toward finding a solution. No matter how much you run away, the test is always going to be there. Running away is is only going to make the problem go away for a little while. Eventually, it will come back worse than ever.

How Do I Tackle Test Anxiety?

Test anxiety is a very powerful feeling. When students feel anxious, they feel weak and helpless. They feel there is nothing they can do to stop their worries. When this happens, anxiety takes over their minds and bodies, leaving them feeling like they are going to lose the test anxiety battle for sure.

Good news: there are many simple things you can do to win the battle over test anxiety! These skills are not hard to learn, and you can even start using them today. Once you learn how to control your anxiety, you are on the road to success in middle school and for all other challenges in your life.

Change the way you think.
Have you ever sat down and thought about how you think? Most of us don't think about how we think; we just go along thinking our thoughts, and we never really consider whether they are helpful or not helpful. We don't realize the way we think has a great deal to do with how we get along in our lives. Our thoughts can influence how we feel about ourselves, how we get along with other people, how well we do in school, and our success on tests. You can learn to have your thoughts chase away the "test-anxiety monster."

It's all how we look at things.

Most seventh graders have heard a parent or a teacher tell them, "There is more than one side to any story." Have you ever considered how you think about different situations?

Take a can of pop and put it on your kitchen table at home. Then, get out a piece of paper and a pen or a pencil. Draw a line down the middle of the paper to divide the paper into two columns. In one column, put the heading: "All the bad things about this can of pop." In the other column, put another heading: "All the good things about this can of pop." Set up your paper like the one below. Here are some answers given by another seventh-grade student.

All the bad things about this can of pop	All the good things about this can of pop
Not an attractive color	Easy-to-read lettering
It's getting warm	Nice to have something to drink
Not much in the can	Inexpensive
Has a lot of sugar	Recyclable aluminum cans

Now look at this chart! It is just as easy to think of good things as it is to think of bad things. Doesn't the same thing hold true for tests? Tests are not good or bad in themselves; they are just a way to challenge us and to see what we know. Tests are stressful, but they are also rewarding. They are hard, but they also make us proud. They make us study often, but we have learned much when we are done. We challenge ourselves, but we also learn we can be successful. We spend time away from our families studying, but later on, we get attention for our efforts. See, there are always two sides to every story!

Avoid all or nothing thinking.

Imagine you had a birthday party. You looked forward to this party for months, knowing you would invite all of your friends and would have a lot of fun. Given that this was your first birthday as a teenager, you were convinced it was going to be the best birthday ever. You invited seventeen friends to your house and had all kinds of activities planned. This would be a birthday party that would go down in history! When your birthday finally came, it was a fun day; however, it was not a perfect day. Two of your friends could not come to your party. You also wanted to set up your stereo speakers outside so everyone could dance, but it rained and everyone had to stay in the house or the garage. Worse than that, your dog started licking your birthday cake. The day was good, but it wasn't "wonderful." After everyone left, you felt let down. Why? Because you expected your birthday to be perfect and it wasn't. Instead of looking at all the wonderful things that happened on your special day, you felt sad because it was not everything you planned in your mind.

Trouble can come when you think a test is going to be either "awful" or "wonderful." If you feel the test is going to be "awful," that will most likely be your experience. You will think all sorts of problem thoughts, and by the time you get to the test, you will be worried, anxious, and even mad. Problems can also happen if you think a test will be "the easiest thing in the world." If you expect to do perfectly, you will find yourself getting more and more worried during the test. Few people know the answer to every question, and no one is perfect. Instead, the test (like your birthday party) is somewhere in the middle. It's not all bad, and it's not all good; it's just a test. Having "all or nothing thinking" is going to get you nowhere. Successful and happy students know that some experiences are better than others, but they try to look at things from all sides.

Don't mind read.

Students who are anxious about tests think they can read the minds of their parents and teachers. These students are convinced that if they do poorly, everyone will think they are "dumb" or "lazy." As they think of all the terrible things people might say about them, they become more anxious. This does not help them do well on tests.

Be careful not to catastrophize.

When people catastrophize, they make everything a catastrophe! A catastrophe is a disaster. People use the word catastrophe to describe a terrible situation. A student who catastrophizes thinks the worst is going to happen. The FCAT is not like a disaster movie! Thinking this test is going to be the worst experience of your life and is going to ruin your future is catastrophizing! Don't do this to yourself! No test is horrible enough to ruin your life. Don't jump to conclusions, because everything will be OK.

Making "should" statements doesn't help!

Every seventh grader should be responsible, but no one can be perfect. Students make themselves anxious when they think they "should" do everything! They feel they "should" be as smart as everyone else, they "should" study more, and they "should" not feel anxious about tests. All these thoughts are pretty ridiculous!

Instead of worrying about being perfect, it is better to set some goals for yourself and to reach them. If you set some reasonable goals for yourself, you will do better on tests. What are reasonable goals? Some seventh graders feel they need to study for a certain amount of time every day to stay on top of their schoolwork. Other students feel they must practice some FCAT questions every day or every week to do their best. Be sure to give yourself time to do other things besides schoolwork to remain a happy and confident person. You and your parents or teachers can work together as a team to find what methods help you do your best.

Replace anxious thoughts with positive thoughts.

Good thoughts (positive thoughts) and bad thoughts (negative thoughts) simply do not go together! If you are thinking something positive, it is almost impossible to think of something negative at the same time. Keep this in mind when test anxiety starts to become a bother.

Even people who are facing some very scary situations can be helped by using positive imagery. Positive imagery is thinking good thoughts to replace anxious thoughts. Positive imagery works to calm people down in any type of situation, such as going to the dentist or having a medical test. You can also use positive imagery to help combat test anxiety. There are two types of thoughts that you can use to make yourself feel less anxious during a testing situation.

- **Thoughts of success.**
  Thinking "I can do it" thoughts chases away thoughts of failure. Think about times you were successful, such as doing well on the soccer field or in a dance recital or helping your mom or dad. Telling yourself you have been a good learner in the past can chase away the test-anxiety monster.

- **Relaxing thoughts.**
  Some people find thinking calming or relaxing thoughts is helpful. Think about a time when you swam in the ocean, had a picnic in the sun, or skateboarded all afternoon. Some seventh graders find listening to music the morning of the test helps them relax. These types of thoughts and activities will get in the way of worry and anxiety and will help you stay focused on positive imagery.

Relax your body as well as your mind!

Just as you can calm your mind, it is also important to relax your body. When students have test anxiety, their muscles become stiff and tense. This causes them to shake, to sweat, to have headaches and stomachaches, and to lose their concentration. If you take deep breaths before a test, letting them out slowly and relaxing your muscles, you will find you will feel much calmer and more confident. This works best when you squeeze or tighten one part of your body at a time and then slowly relax it while breathing deeply and calmly. Your school counselor will probably have many more ideas about relaxing your body. He or she might even suggest that everyone in your class learn to relax in this way. Learning how to calm your body down helps in school, in sports, and in generally feeling healthy.

Don't let yourself feel alone.

Everyone feels anxious when they feel alone and separate from others. Talk to your friends, parents, and teachers about your feelings. You may be surprised to find that your really good friends understand what you are going through. They probably feel worried and anxious at times as well. Your parents and teachers also care and are there to help you. You will find that when you talk, not only will you feel better, but you will get lots of ideas and help from other people.

Be sure to take care of yourself!

Seventh grade is a busy year. It is easy to forget to eat breakfast or to not sleep enough. Eating and sleeping right are important, especially before a test like the FCAT. When we do not eat right, this makes us have a hard time paying attention. Being tired does not help either. Try to get in the habit of going to bed an hour earlier several nights before the FCAT. You want to feel fresh, awake, and ready to beat that test-anxiety monster! Be sure to find a morning routine which works for you. Make sure you get up on time so you do not feel rushed the morning of a test. You may want to ask your parents to help you stick to your morning routine, especially on the morning of a test.

Practice your test-taking success.

People who have accomplished incredibly difficult goals have used their imaginations to help them be successful. They thought about what they would do step by step to be successful. You can do the same! Think about yourself on the morning of the test. Imagine thinking positive thoughts and eating a good breakfast. Think about arriving at school and feeling sure you will do fine on the test. Imagine closing your eyes before the test, breathing deeply, and relaxing. Think about all the good strategies you have learned to help you do well on the FCAT. The more you program your mind to think in a positive way, the more calm, confident, and successful you will be.

Learn to use study skills.

There is a chapter in this book that will help you learn test-taking strategies. The more you know about taking tests successfully, the calmer you will feel. Knowledge is power! It may take some time to learn test-taking strategies, but it is worth the effort! If you can study well and beat the test-anxiety monster, you will be amazed at how well you can do! You will be ready to show what you know.

Congratulate yourself during the test.

Instead of thinking, "I've only done five problems, and I've got pages to go," or "I knew three answers, but one mixed me up," reward yourself for what you have done. Tell yourself, "I got some answers right so far, so I bet I can do more." After every success on the test, take a second to tell yourself, "I really <u>can</u> do this stuff." This will help you maintain positive thoughts and give you your best chance to succeed on the test.

Conclusion

In this chapter, you have read about many different ways to help combat test anxiety. It is important for you to find which strategies work best for you and continue to use them. You are the only person who can decide what you need to do in order to show what you know on tests.

Test-Taking Strategies

How to Show What You Know on Tests!

No one ever said seventh grade was going to be easy! If you think your classes are harder, homework never seems to leave you alone, and you have to study harder for tests, you are probably right!

So what can you do to be more successful in school? Studying and paying attention in class both really help you to be a whiz at tests; but you can do better than you thought on any test at school, including the Florida Comprehensive Assessment Test (FCAT), by learning to use some simple test-taking tools. Everyone needs good tools (another name for tools is "strategies") when facing a problem. Without the right tools, even the smartest people will never be able to show what they know. You could be a brilliant surgeon and know everything there is to know about the human body, but will you really save the patient if your scalpel isn't sharpened? Remember, studying hard and using test-taking strategies will lead you to test-taking success.

It's Not Hard to Be a Star!

Here are some tools you can use on the FCAT and any other tests you have to take.

Be an active learner.

Wouldn't it be great if you could learn everything you needed to know to do well on the FCAT by just sitting in class? All you would have to do is sit in your seat and stay awake. Like magic, you would be a genius! Sadly, learning does not work this way. Instead, you have to pay attention, have to think about what is being said in class, and have to participate during the school day. This will make you an "active learner." Active learners enjoy school, learn more, feel good about themselves, and usually do better on tests.

Being an active learner takes time and practice. If you are the type of student who is easily bored or frustrated, it is going to take some practice to use your classroom time differently. Ask yourself the following questions.

- Am I looking at the teachers?
- Do I pay attention to what is being said?
- Do I have any questions or ideas about what the teacher is saying?
- Do I listen to what my fellow students are saying and think about their ideas?
- Do I work with others to try to solve difficult problems?
- Do I look at the clock and wonder what time school will be over, or do I appreciate what is happening during the school day and how much I can learn?
- Do I try to think about how my schoolwork might be helpful now or in the future?

The more you listen, think, and participate, the better your FCAT scores will be.

Read the directions carefully!

One of the worst mistakes a student can make on the FCAT is to ignore directions or to read directions carelessly. By the time you are a seventh grader, you probably think you have heard every direction ever invented. This makes it very easy for you to "tune out" directions, but that would be a very bad idea!

Taking the time to read and to understand directions and questions is a great test-taking skill! On the 7th-Grade FCAT, directions are not always simple. Sometimes, directions have more than one part to them. Read the question slowly and read it twice! Reading questions too quickly or reading them only one time can cause mistakes. If you read directions too quickly, there is a good chance you will not understand what is being asked. When we hurry, we tend to skip over words or to get confused about what is being asked. For example, if you are looking at a graph that shows the heights of all mountains in South America and you are asked which peak is the lowest, it would be easy to read the question incorrectly and think you are being asked which peak is the highest. You might be an expert at graphs, but if you are not an expert at reading questions, you will never show what you know!

Know how to fill in the answer bubbles!

When you ask most seventh graders if they know about answer bubbles, they will probably tell you that is a silly question. Most seventh graders have already had a great deal of experience at filling in answer bubbles on tests. Unfortunately, sometimes it is easy to forget you have to fill in the answer bubble <u>darkly</u> or your answer will not be counted. If you write too lightly, or use a check mark or a dot, even if you found the correct answer, no one will ever know. Remember, a computer will be scoring your multiple-choice questions.

On the Mathematics test for the FCAT, filling in answer bubbles gets a little more complicated with the addition of gridded-response questions. It is very important that you take time to study and to practice filling in the response grid so you know what to do in a testing situation. Don't forget there are **answer boxes** and **number bubbles**. Answer boxes are boxes where you write your answer, and number bubbles are the gridded answer bubbles where you fill in the correct answer. Be sure to read more information about gridded responses on page vi in this book.

Map out the information given to you in the question.

Now that you know you should read directions and questions carefully and fill in answer bubbles correctly, it is time to think about the whole FCAT test. One of the best things you can do to have the best test score possible is to get to know the FCAT. There are two types of questions on the 7th-Grade FCAT: multiple-choice and gridded-response. Knowing what type of answer is needed for each question type will help you begin to think about how to express your answer. (See page vi for a thorough description of each question type.)

After you figure out what type of question is being asked, you need to think about the content of the question. Think about the FCAT Reading test. On that test, you will be given items to read, and then you will be asked questions about what you have read. Sometimes, you will be asked to read material that is fiction, while at other times the material is nonfiction. If the story seems like a fiction story to you, start thinking about what types of questions you might be asked. If the story is fiction, you are probably going to be asked questions about the meaning of the story. If the reading material is scientific or historical, you might be asked facts about the material, or you might have to think about what you read in a logical or scientific manner. If you are able to get an idea about what type of material you are reading, you will get a better idea about what types of questions you might be asked. This tool will help give you a head start in figuring out the correct answer.

Check to see if there are any diagrams, maps, graphs, or other drawings or illustrations with the story or question. Take a quick look at those. What type of illustration is there? The type of illustration might make a difference in the questions you are going to be asked. For example, if you see a bar graph as part of a question, you probably will be asked a "how much" question. If you see a shape with measurements, you might be asked a question about a size or area.

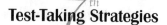

Don't speed through the test!

It is a very bad idea to rush through the FCAT. The purpose of the FCAT is to find out how much you know, not how fast you can work! The FCAT gives students plenty of time to do their best on the test.

Taking practice tests gives you a good idea of how long it takes you to finish certain sections of the FCAT. Once you feel comfortable with the FCAT, you will be able to make better use of your time. This is why taking FCAT practice tests is a very helpful test-taking tool.

Don't forget to use the mathematics reference sheet and a calculator!

For the Reading FCAT, the only tools you will be allowed to use are the test-taking strategies you develop. On the Mathematics FCAT, however, you will be given a calculator and a mathematics reference sheet to use. It is important to understand how to use these tools and when to use them. Practice using a calculator to do math. Know what operations you can use it for. **Always** check your own math with the calculator. It is also important to know how to use the reference sheet to your advantage. If you know what is on that sheet, you can remember to use that information in solving mathematics problems; otherwise, it is just a meaningless piece of paper with numbers and lines on it. Remember, the purpose of the Mathematics test is to show how well you can think, not how much you can memorize. The calculator and the reference sheet are tools to help you succeed. Learn how to use them!

Don't get stuck on one question.

When taking a test like the FCAT, nothing seems worse than getting stuck on one question. You stare and stare at that question, but the answer just isn't there! The more you stare, the worse you feel, and the more you worry. Before you know it, you are out of time.

Questions on the FCAT will be harder for some seventh graders than for others, and very few seventh graders in the state will get every question correct on the FCAT. So, if you think a couple of questions are hard, you are not alone. Tell yourself it is OK to move on from hard a question. One missed answer will not ruin your FCAT score. Put a mark by a question that you are not able to figure out and come back to the question later. Sometimes taking a break gives you a chance to relax. Suddenly, the answer pops into your mind! Also, if you spend too much time worrying about a question you don't know how to do, you are preventing yourself from moving on to other questions that you find easy. It's better to get one wrong answer and to move on to get the next thirty questions right than to struggle with one question so long that you only are able to do ten more questions. Tell yourself it is OK not to know everything, move on to another question, and you will do great on the FCAT.

Always recheck your work!

Most students feel rechecking work takes too much time and is boring. Who wants to do the same work again? However, rechecking your work does not mean you have to do the problem all over again. Just looking at a question and your answer for a few seconds can make the difference between a right and wrong answer. Read the following hints to see how.

- **Is your work neat?**

Neatness counts! Although you will not lose points if your work is messy, messy work can be a problem for you in many ways. You can make mistakes in your mathematical calculations if your writing is messy or careless. It is easy to mistake one number for another or to line up your columns of addition, subtraction, or multiplication unevenly. If any numbers stand out to you as messy or unreadable, make sure you wrote down what you really meant and recheck your calculations. A "0" that looks like a "6" or a "÷" that looks like a "–" can also lead to a wrong answer. The messier your writing, the more chances for making a mistake.

- **Does the answer make sense?**

Take a good look at the information presented and at what you are being asked. Is your answer at least a good estimate of what the correct response might be? For example, you might answer that the distance between Miami and Fort Lauderdale is 50 feet. When you think about it, does that make sense? Fifty feet is not far at all! Instead, the answer is probably closer to 50 **miles**. You should have had the right answer, but it's now wrong because you mistakenly wrote the wrong unit.

- **Make sure you have not filled in two different answer bubbles for a single question.**

For multiple-choice questions, each question has only one answer. Be sure you do not mark two bubbles on the same question. When answering gridded-response questions, make sure each number column has only one bubble filled in and that the number corresponds to the number written above it in the answer boxes. Every so often, take a look at your answers to be sure you are filling them in correctly. Are there any extra marks? If so, go back and correct your mistake.

Answer every question.

On multiple-choice questions, you have a one out of four chance of getting a question right, even if you just close your eyes and guess! That means for every four questions you guess, the odds are that you will get about 25% (one out of four) of the answers right. Guessing alone is not going to make you a star on the FCAT, but leaving multiple-choice questions blank is not going to help you either. If you ever come to a question that makes no sense, just take a guess. You have nothing to lose and everything to gain.

Power guessing is a useful form of guessing. Power guessing means using all you know to sort out answers that possibly could be right or wrong. Not everything you know was learned in the classroom. Part of what everyone knows comes from just living every day. When you take the FCAT, you should use everything you learned in school, but you should also use your experiences outside the classroom to help answer questions correctly. Using your common sense as well as other information you know will help you do especially well on the FCAT.

Some students use a code to rate each answer when they feel they might have to guess. Don't forget you are allowed to write in your test booklet! In fact, it is a very good idea to write in your test booklet to help you make better choices. Using your pencil, you can mark the following codes beside each multiple-choice answer choice to see what would make the best guess.

(+) Putting a "plus sign" by your answer means you are not sure if this answer is correct, but you think this answer is probably more likely to be correct than the others.

(?) Putting a "question mark" by your answer means you are unsure if this is the correct answer, but you don't want to rule it out completely.

(–) Putting a "minus sign" by your answer means you are pretty sure this is the wrong answer. You would then choose from the other answers to make an educated guess.

As previously mentioned, before you even read a question, you have a one out of four chance of getting it right. Think how your chances improve when you use power guessing and codes to help you answer questions. If you can eliminate one of the choices using these strategies, you will have a one in three chance of getting the answer right; if you are able to eliminate two of the choices, you now have a 50% chance of getting it right! You've doubled your chances of guessing it correctly, and that doesn't even take into account any knowledge you can apply to the question! This is useful information when you come to a question that stumps you. As previously stated, it is not good to let yourself get stuck on a question. If you remind yourself you have a good chance of just guessing the correct answer for a question you're unsure about, you will be able to move on more quickly to questions you do know how to answer without using any guessing strategies.

Pay attention to yourself and not to others.

When you are a seventh grader, you will probably find yourself paying more attention to your friends and classmates. Most seventh graders wonder and worry about what other people are wearing, what the latest gossip is, and who is friends with whom. All this is an important part of the life of a seventh grader, but how you do on the FCAT has nothing to do with how others do on the FCAT. This is your own test and your own challenge! When taking the FCAT, you need to concentrate on what you are doing, not what others around you are doing. Looking around the room, trying to see what page of the test your friends are working on, or trying to judge how they are feeling is only going to waste your time. Pay attention to yourself. Concentrate on the test. It pays off!

Take a little break!

Taking a test can be stressful. Most seventh graders will probably tell you there are many other things they would rather do than take a test. If you feel worried, stressed, or bored when you are taking a test, give yourself a little break (remember, you will have plenty of time to finish the test, so if you need a break, take one). Close your eyes for a second or two, take a deep breath, and try to relax. Stretch your arms and feet. Think a positive thought about yourself, such as, "I'm a smart kid. I'm sure I can do great on this test." Think about something you have accomplished in your life, such as scoring a goal or helping your dad paint the house. You will soon feel better and will be able to return to the test and show what you know!

Reading

Introduction

The Reading section of the 7th Grade Florida Comprehensive Assessment Test (FCAT) measures how well you understand what you read. You will read stories and informational texts. Then, you will answer questions about what you read. You might be asked to tell what the main idea of a story is or to tell the meaning of a word. The questions will ask you to pick the right answer from four choices. The reading questions are written clearly and are not meant to trick you.

The Reading chapter has two sections. In the first section, you will complete 20 practice items that will help you practice your test-taking skills. After these practice items, there is a sample assessment test which has been created to be like the real Reading FCAT. You cannot use outside reference materials to help you answer questions.

Practice Items

Read the story "Pick a Card" before answering questions 1 and 2.

Pick a Card

Cyril slammed his locker shut. He hoped the noise was loud enough to bother the coach. He hoped the coach had a headache.

"You guys, hurry up!" shouted Coach Mike. "I need to see some enthusiastic players today!" The coach walked through the locker room. He handed each boy a card as he walked by. Cyril's card said "IS TODAY THE DAY?" in plain, capital letters. Cyril slid the card into his sock and looked toward the field. "Let's go! Let's go! Let's go! We're starting in fifteen!"

There were only a few weeks until the first game of the season, and Cyril ached to prove that he deserved to be on this team. Despite his best efforts, it had seemed as though Coach Mike hardly believed in him.

"Extra pushups, extra sit-ups, extra laps," thought Cyril as he suited up. "He's always asking more of me. Why do I have to try so hard? He's so much easier on other kids, especially his favorites."

Cyril was one of the last players to make it out of the locker room. Across the field, he saw Miguel sitting on the bench, alone. He was studying his playbook. The two were friends, but Cyril couldn't help but feel some resentment. He walked across the grass and threw his helmet on the bench.

"Hey," said Cyril. "What's your card say?"

"Who cares," muttered Miguel in a bitter voice. He barely took his eyes off the pages.

"Just wondered what Coach gave his favorite player," Cyril quipped as he took a seat next to the quarterback. Although Cyril was teasing his friend, he was serious about the favoritism.

Miguel gave Cyril a quizzical look. "Have you been practicing with your eyes closed? Great, Cyril."

"If you ask Coach, he'll tell you I am great at one thing: not trying hard enough."

"What?" Miguel didn't believe what he had just heard. "That's the kind of stuff he's been telling me. 'Miguel, you didn't give it your best yesterday. Miguel, I can't count on you after a practice like that.' "

"Are you serious?" Cyril was taken aback by what he had just heard. "Has Coach been feeding everyone this stuff?"

"I guess," Miguel shrugged. "So what card did he give you?"

Cyril pulled the card from his sock. "Is today the day?" he uttered as he ripped the card into pieces. Slowly, it drifted like confetti to the grass below.

Base your answers to questions 1 and 2 on the story "Pick a Card."

1. Read this sentence from the story.

   "Just wondered what Coach gave his favorite player," Cyril quipped as he took a seat next to the quarterback.

   What does the word *quipped* mean?

   ○ A. to say something happily
   ○ B. to say something sarcastically
   ○ C. to say something angrily
   ○ D. to say something sadly

2. Read this sentence from the story.

   Miguel gave Cyril a quizzical look.

   Why did Miguel give Cyril a *quizzical* look?

   ○ F. Miguel did not want to believe what Cyril had said.
   ○ G. Miguel did not hear what Cyril had said.
   ○ H. Miguel was surprised by what Cyril had said.
   ○ I. Miguel was not listening to Cyril.

The Grand Canyon

The Grand Canyon, an especially vast canyon located in northwestern Arizona, is 277 miles long. It starts at a point known as Lees Ferry and ends at Grand Wash Cliffs. The average width of the canyon is about 10 miles; this measure is rarely uniform, however. Its widest section is about 18 miles wide, while its narrowest section stretches approximately 5 miles across. Similarly, the depth of this great chasm is not always consistent. It's nearly a vertical mile (about 5,000 feet) from the tip of the South Rim to the bottom where the Colorado River flows below. At its deepest, the canyon boasts a 6,000-foot vertical expanse.

This amazing geological attraction has three distinct sections: the North Rim, the South Rim, and the Inner Canyon. Although each is part of the Grand Canyon, there is a great difference among climates. On average, 26 inches of precipitation fall at the North Rim, while the South Rim only receives around 16 inches each year. The Inner Canyon experiences even less precipitation. The descent into the Inner Canyon moves one closer to the desert. The increased depth results in hotter temperatures and drier conditions. The temperature at the bottom exceeds the temperature above by about 35° F.

Much of the Inner Canyon is considered desert, with the exception of the areas along the Colorado River and its tributary streams. The high summer temperature in the belly of the canyon can reach 120° F. Much of the sparse vegetation is similar to that which can be found in the deserts of the southern United States, including cacti and drought-resistant shrubs.

The forests along the rim sharply contrast the arid[1] conditions of the area below. Ponderosa pines are prevalent[2], as are pinyon pines, gambles oaks, and Utah junipers. These trees have adapted to the extreme conditions faced by the regions above the rim, including torrential spring rains, bone-dry summers, and winters full of snowstorms. While these extreme environments are more likely found along the North Rim, the South Rim does experience such conditions on a milder scale.

A view from the Inner Canyon

[1]**arid**: dry
[2]**prevalent**: common

Base your answers to questions 3 through 5 on the article "The Grand Canyon."

3. How does the climate of the Inner Canyon compare with the climates of the regions above the rim?

   ○ A. The Inner Canyon is warmer and receives more precipitation than regions above the rim.
   ○ B. The Inner Canyon is warmer and drier than regions above the rim.
   ○ C. The Inner Canyon and the regions above the rim receive the same amount precipitation.
   ○ D. The Inner Canyon is colder and receives more precipitation than regions above the rim.

4. Which of the following statements is accurate?

   ○ F. Ponderosa pines and Utah junipers are common in the Inner Canyon.
   ○ G. The climate at the South Rim is more extreme than the North Rim's climate.
   ○ H. The Inner Canyon and the deserts of the southern United States have similar plant life.
   ○ I. The entire area known as the Inner Canyon is considered a desert.

5. How does the depth of the South Rim compare with the Grand Canyon's deepest point?

   ○ A. The South Rim is the deepest point of the Grand Canyon.
   ○ B. The deepest point of the Grand Canyon is about 1,000 feet deeper than the South Rim.
   ○ C. The deepest point of the Grand Canyon is about 6,000 feet deep, while the depth at the South Rim is exactly 1,000 feet.
   ○ D. The deepest point of the Grand Canyon measures one vertical mile longer than the depth of the South Rim.

Read the story "The Gifted Chef" before answering questions 6 through 8.

The Gifted Chef

In Juanita's family, everyone has to cook dinner one night a week. She, her two brothers, and her parents alternate nights. The other two nights are reserved for leftovers. On special occasions, they order pizza or go out to a restaurant. Juanita's night to cook is Tuesday. She's been doing this since she was just six years old. At that time, she needed a little more help as she prepared spaghetti or sandwiches. With weekly practice and a few years of experience under her belt, Juanita has grown more confident. These days, Tuesday nights mean more complex meals. Juanita experiments with her own recipes and keeps a special notebook of hits and misses. Her brothers are quick to tell her how each Tuesday night meal should be categorized.

As a member of Junior Chefs, Juanita frequently submits her unique recipes in local cooking contests. She has even won a few awards, but each of these contests only required one recipe. The upcoming Gifted Chef Quest means preparing a three-course meal. The rules call for entries in three categories: soup, salad, and entrée.

The Gifted Chef Quest brings together teens from all over the city. While many would like to enter, the Quest requires a first place finish in one of the local contests it sponsors. This year, there are 12 contestants who meet the requirement. Each is vying[1] for the top prize. All the aspiring[2] teenage chefs can think of no better reward than the summer job as a chef's assistant.

Four teens will prepare their meals each night. Monday through Wednesday, a group of eight judges will taste each contestant's fare[3], giving a score for each category. The judges will dine on a sample only, so as not to get too full. Therefore, the chefs need to make sure their entries are memorable. Additionally, the teen chefs will receive points for presentation. Thursday has been reserved for the awards presentation.

Juanita arrives for the Gifted Chef Quest around 4:00 p.m. on Tuesday. She carries two grocery bags filled with her ingredients. Her backpack contains eight hand-written menus, her special notebook, and a collection of utensils. While the Gifted Chef Quest provides many different kitchen gadgets and appliances, there are a few tools Juanita can't live without. They clatter in her pack with each step.

A chalkboard with her name on it hangs over her workstation. The kitchen is already humming with the sounds of three other contestants. Each wears a white smock⁴ similar to Juanita's. She smiles and chats for a moment or two but is quick to focus on the task ahead of her. She places her tools and the bags' contents on the counter; preparation doesn't begin until the bell rings.

At the 4:20 p.m. tone, Juanita gets to work. She puts a pot of water, a copper saucepan, and a black, cast-iron frying pan on the stove. Someone from the Gifted Chef Quest helps her with the burners. While all that's heating, it's time for cold cucumber soup. She carefully peels and dices several cucumbers. "I'm sure glad I have my own stuff here," she thinks. Into the blender the pieces go along with plain yogurt, sour cream, salt, and freshly squeezed lemon juice. With the snap of the lid and a touch of the purée button, the soup is on its way. She pours the light green treat into four bowls.

She needs the blender for her salad dressing. Juanita gives it a thorough rinsing in the kitchen sink and starts the salad and its dressing. The blender now holds a combination of raspberries and secret ingredients. The focused chef mixes her dressing and transfers it into a small pitcher. Next, she dries two bunches of fresh spinach leaves and lines four plates with green piles. Juanita sprinkles each with crushed walnuts and crumbled blue cheese. Just before serving this course, Juanita will top her salads with fresh cut apple slices and her secret raspberry dressing.

Without stopping to think, Juanita moves back to the stove. Tonight, the judges will be enjoying sautéed chicken over pasta in lemon-butter sauce. Pats of butter melt as soon as they hit the pans. Lightly floured chicken is lowered into the frying pan. The sizzling adds to the commotion in the kitchen. Another half-stick of butter melts in the saucepan; Juanita adds half a can of chicken broth and the juice of a few lemons. She whisks in her special ingredients and lowers the heat so the sauce can thicken. The chicken is turned, and a golden brown crust lets Juanita know her entrée's main ingredient is coming along nicely.

Luckily, the pasta doesn't have to be homemade. Juanita throws long, thin pasta noodles into the pot's boiling water. It only takes a few minutes for the pasta to cook. She drains the noodles and spoons the long pieces of steaming pasta onto the judges' plates. The finished chicken is placed on its noodle bed. Each plate is topped with the lemon-butter sauce. Juanita sprinkles each entrée with some fresh chopped parsley. She finishes off the salad preparation and crosses her fingers. "This is it!" The kitchen door opens as Juanita makes her way to the judges' table to present her menu.

¹**vying**: competing
²**aspiring**: hopeful
³**fare**: meal
⁴**smock**: coat-like garment

Base your answers to questions 6 through 8 on the story "The Gifted Chef."

6.   Which of the following sentences summarizes this story?

   ○ F.   Juanita hopes to win the Gifted Chef Quest contest.
   ○ G.   A young chef prepares a unique menu for a cooking contest.
   ○ H.   Juanita has been cooking on Tuesday nights since she was six years old.
   ○ I.   A young chef wins a cooking contest with her special lemon-butter chicken and pasta entrée.

7.   Why does Juanita want to win the Gifted Chef Quest contest?

   ○ A.   She wants to win the special trophy.
   ○ B.   She wants her recipes to be published in a cookbook.
   ○ C.   She wants to work as a chef's assistant during the summer.
   ○ D.   She wants to be a famous chef someday.

8.   Why is Juanita qualified to participate in the Gifted Chef Quest contest?

   ○ F.   Juanita has been cooking since she was six years old.
   ○ G.   Juanita makes up her own recipes.
   ○ H.   Juanita was selected by the judges of the Gifted Chef Quest to participate.
   ○ I.   Juanita won a local cooking contest sponsored by the Gifted Chef Quest.

Read the article "No Laughing Matter for Local Theater" before answering questions 9 through 11.

No Laughing Matter for Local Theater

SMITHVILLE—These days, supporters of the Downtown Theater have all but given up hope of reopening the treasured landmark. The Smithville Historical Society has been unable to raise the nearly $2 million required to bring the theater up to code. According to city inspector Carrie Owens, "The Downtown Theater has electrical and structural problems. I'm worried that turning on all the lights will send sparks flying through the wooden structure. That's a fire hazard. And the roof; it's only a matter of time before it caves in."

The theater, best known for showcasing some of the best comedians in the state, closed its doors six months ago. "Before the city stepped in, proceeds from daily ticket sales made it possible for me to keep the doors open," says theater owner Don Murphy. "Then I got the city's renovation[1] bill. I just couldn't save enough to make a dent in the repairs. I had to turn off the lights and close the doors. A lot of time has passed since then, and I was hoping our partnership with the Historical Society would help, but it doesn't look good."

Over the past half year, the Smithville Historical Society has worked to raise funds for the renovation. Five months ago, the group tried to have the 150-year-old theater declared a city landmark. Such a title would make city funding available to the theater. According to city bylaws, however, the significant remodeling to the exterior of the building in the 1950s and to the stage in the 1960s makes the theater ineligible for landmark status.

Upon hearing the request for landmark status had been turned down, the Historical Society took another approach. A benefit comedy showcase was planned, but Owens refused the request to open the theater for the day-long event. She cited the dangers to which the ticket holders would have been exposed. "I know it was only one day, but I couldn't in good conscience let the society open the doors. What if something would have happened? I don't want anyone to be in harm's way, even for a good cause," says Owens.

Only a handful of the ticket holders demanded a refund when the show didn't go on. Most, including downtown resident Phil Garcia, saw the ticket price as a donation. "I was hoping we could get this theater up and running. It was such a great place. I was happy to donate my ticket price. I wish I could give more." While many in the community have similar feelings, the donations resulting from showcase ticket sales only amounted to $100,000.

Early in the fundraising process, things looked promising for the Downtown Theater supporters. The Historical Society received an anonymous pledge of $500,000 if the remaining $1,500,000 was raised. "I was so happy when that call came into my office," says Smithville Historical Society President Alice Kim, "I almost fell off my chair." The pledge inspired the society to dedicate part of its own budget to the project, bringing total funds raised during the first three months of effort to $1,000,000.

"Since then, everything seems to have stalled," says Kim. There is a great deal of enthusiasm among Smithville residents when it comes to reopening the theater's door, but money from the community residents has only trickled in. "We haven't been able to get anything going in the last three months, and renovations can't start until the entire sum is raised. I wish there was more we could do for Mr. Murphy, for the theater, and for those who want to sit in the audience again. As long as there are people who remember the theater's greatness, there are going to be dreamers such as myself hoping it will reopen. I'll do what I can to make sure my dream, and theirs, comes true."

¹**renovation**: repair

Base your answers to questions 9 through 11 on the article "No Laughing Matter for Local Theater."

9.   Why did the author write this article?

   ○ A. to entertain readers with a story about a popular theater known for its comedy shows
   ◑ B. to describe the problems the Smithville Historical Society has had trying to raise money to repair the Downtown Theater
   ○ C. to describe the problems Downtown Theater owner Don Murphy has had with poor attendance at events
   ○ D. to emphasize the importance of preserving historic landmarks, such as the Downtown Theater

10. Read this sentence from the article.

   There is a great deal of enthusiasm among Smithville residents when it comes to reopening the theater's door, but money from the community residents has only trickled in.

   The author is MOST LIKELY to agree with which of the following statements?

   ◑ F. Most of the Smithville residents have worked hard to raise money to reopen the Downtown Theater.
   ○ G. Although many people would like to see the theater reopen, they are not willing to help cover the cost.
   ○ H. The Smithville Historical Society is not working hard enough to get residents involved in fundraising efforts.
   ○ I. Smithville residents want the theater to reopen, and they are willing to raise funds for the renovation.

11. What is the primary reason the author included information about the pledge of $500,000?

   ◑ A. to emphasize fundraising efforts haven't always seemed as hopeless as the current situation
   ○ B. to emphasize the generosity of all Smithville residents
   ○ C. to inform readers of the exact sources of funds for theater renovations
   ○ D. to inform readers about the problems the Historical Society has had when raising funds

Read the article "Zora Neale Hurston" before answering questions 12 and 13.

Zora Neale Hurston

Zora Neale Hurston was born on January 7, 1891. Zora was raised in Eatonville, Florida, a town with historical significance. It was the first all-black incorporated[1] city in the United States. Zora, a future writer and folklorist[2], was the daughter of a Baptist preacher and a schoolteacher. Unfortunately, Zora's mother died when she was in her early teens. The fifth child of eight, Zora moved in with one of her brothers upon her mother's death. She helped raise her nieces and nephews which left her eager to remove herself from the responsibilities of caring for a household. At age 16, Zora joined a traveling theater company. In addition to her work as a performer, Zora worked as a maid for well-to-do households and pursued an education.

In 1925, Zora headed to New York City. She quickly became an important part of the Harlem Renaissance, an African-American cultural movement of the 1920s and 1930s that brought African-American literature, music, art, and politics to the attention of the American public. Zora was a skilled storyteller. She traveled throughout New York, Florida, and the Caribbean collecting oral histories. She collaborated with Langston Hughes to write a play in 1931, and her first novel, *Jonah's Gourd Vine*, was published in 1934.

Zora's most well-known work, *Their Eyes Were Watching God*, was published in 1937. At that time, the novel was criticized for not taking a political stand against racism and poverty. Instead, Zora chose to focus on her main character's search for love and happiness as a black woman of the South. Today, most people choose to celebrate the novel's rich tradition of the rural black South as presented in Zora's words.

Zora went on to publish several other novels in the 1940s. These books enjoyed modest success, but her writing career eventually declined. Around 1950, she moved back to Florida. She worked as a maid until her health made such chores impossible. She lived out her remaining days penniless and alone. She suffered from a stroke and died in 1959. She was buried in an unmarked grave in Fort Pierce, Florida.

In the 1970s, many of Zora's writings were rediscovered by up-and-coming black writers. With a renewed audience, several of Zora's works were republished. A whole new generation is now able to read Zora's words which address race, gender, and the search for freedom. Today, Zora Neale Hurston is considered one of the most important African-American writers in American history.

[1]**incorporated**: established
[2]**folklorist**: someone who gathers and studies unwritten stories, traditions, and legends

Base your answers to questions 12 and 13 on the article "Zora Neale Hurston."

12. What was the Harlem Renaissance?

   ○ F. a time in American history when hundreds of houses were built in Harlem
   ○ G. a cultural movement that emphasized African-American literature and art
   ○ H. a cultural movement that centered around the literature and art of European nations
   ○ I.   a time in American history when Harlem residents began to build homes

13. Which of the following BEST illustrates Zora Neale Hurston's contribution to American history?

   ○ A. She was an important writer who celebrated African-American culture.
   ○ B. She died penniless and alone.
   ○ C. She wrote a popular novel, *Their Eyes Were Watching God*.
   ○ D. She grew up in the first all-black incorporated city in the United States.

Read O.W. Meier's personal narrative about the Nebraska Blizzard of 1888 before answering questions 12 and 13.

O.W. Meier recalls his experience during the Nebraska Blizzard of 1888.

"The awful blizzard of January 12, 1888," said O. W. Meier, "cannot be forgotten by anyone who experienced it as I did." He and his brothers were attending school in District 71, 15 miles southwest of Lincoln, and this is his story of that blizzard which swept over the country 50 years ago.

"The weather had been mild, after a heavy fall of snow. Deep snow lay over all the ground in fields and on the roads. Long hanging icicles dripped melting snow water from the eaves of the house and barn. The sky was dark and heavy. Beautiful big white flakes were falling fast that morning of the fateful day. Father and mother said, "The girls must stay at home, but the boys may go to school."

"At half past eight Walter, then 8, Henry 12, and I, 15 years of age, started out through the deep white snow. Pretty starry flakes made us look like snowmen before we reached the school, a mile and a half from home. When we got there we found other boys, and some girls, playing "fox and geese." Henry and I joined in the game.

"The bell rang, calling us in to study and to recite. The heavy snow kept falling all that day. By the middle of the afternoon, at the last recess, the snow was about two feet deep, and on the top, it was almost as light as feathers. We rushed for the brooms to sweep the wet snow from our boots. Just when we got settled down to our books, as swiftly as lightning, the storm struck the north side of the house. The whole building shivered and quaked. With a deafening whack, the shutters were slammed shut by the terrific wind. In an instant the room became as black as night, then for a moment there came a ray of light, I stood and said, "May my brothers and I go home?" The teacher said, "Those boys who live south may put on their coats and go, but the rest of you must stay here in this house."

"The two Strelow boys, Robert and George, with John Conrad, my two brothers, and I put out into the storm for our homes. We had not gone a rod when we found ourselves in a heap, in a heavy drift of snow. We took hold of each others' hands, pulled ourselves out, got into the road, and the cold north wind blew us down the road a half mile south, where the Strelow boys and John Conrad had to go west a mile or more.

When they reached a bridge in a ravine, the little fellows sheltered a while under the bridge, a wooden culvert, but Robert, the oldest, insisted that they push on through the blinding storm for their homes. In the darkness they stumbled in, and by degrees their parents thawed them out, bathed their frozen hands, noses, ears and cheeks, while the boys cried in pain.

"My brothers and I could not walk through the deep snow in the road, so we took down the rows of corn stalks to keep from losing ourselves until we reached our pasture fence. Walter was too short to wade the deep snow in the field, so Henry and I dragged him over the top. For nearly a mile we followed the fence until we reached the corral and pens. In the howling storm, we could hear the pigs squeal as they were freezing in the mud and snow. Sister Ida had opened the gate and let the cows in from the field to the sheds, just as the cold wind struck and froze her skirt stiff around her like a hoop. The barn and stables were drifted over when we reached there. The roaring wind and stifling snow blinded us so that we had to feel through the yard to the door of our house.

"The lamp was lighted. Mother was walking the floor, wringing her hands and calling for her boys. Pa was shaking the ice and snow from his coat and boots. He had gone out to meet us but was forced back by the storm. We stayed in the house all that night. It was so cold that many people froze to death in the snow, and the loss in livestock was big. The next morning we walked out upon the hard, deep drifts and shoveled a way through to the barn. We found our cows and horses alive on top of the snow that had drifted into their stalls, but a lot of our hogs were frozen stiff in mud, ice and snow. The road we came over on our way home was strewn with frozen quails and rabbits.

"That was an awful night on the open plains. Many teachers and school children lost their lives in that blinding storm, while trying to find their way home. The blizzard of 1888 has not been forgotten."

source: Library of Congress, Manuscript Division, Works Projects Administration (formerly Works Progress Administration), Federal Writers' Project Collection

Base your answers to questions 14 and 15 on O.W. Meier's personal narrative.

14. Why is O.W. Meier qualified to speak on the events of the Blizzard of 1888?

    ○ F. O.W. Meier experienced the blizzard first hand.
    ○ G. O.W. Meier's mother told him about the blizzard.
    ○ H. O.W. Meier studied the blizzard's events in school.
    ○ I.   O.W. Meier interviewed someone who lived through the Blizzard of 1888.

15. Which of the following statements gives the BEST evidence that the Blizzard of 1888 negatively impacted the town of Lincoln, Nebraska?

    ○ A. O.W. Meier said the town was hurt by the blizzard.
    ○ B. O.W. Meier recalled many people died as a result of the blizzard.
    ○ C. O.W. Meier's mother was concerned about the effects of the blizzard.
    ○ D. O.W. Meier's teacher let children go home early from school because of the blizzard.

Base your answers to questions 16 through 18 on the poem "Something to See."

Something to See
Pieces of paper swirl and twist in the wind,
brushing past storefronts and over cracks in the sidewalk.
They do a pretty good job of keeping pace with me.
I wonder where they came from
and to whom they once belonged.
Their former owners star in mini daydreams, but
when I round the corner, I lose my companions.
The southward breeze takes them on a different course.

The sun shines down through tall buildings.
I look to the left, then glance up.
Structures of glass and steel stretch to the sky.
The right side of the street is the same.
I like having these pillars on either side.
They keep everyone moving in the right direction.

My feet carefully navigate wads of gum no longer distinguishable as such.
They look like little black circles against the cement trail.
Every once in awhile, my tennis shoe gets caught
because I'm paying attention to other things.
When that happens, I feel the sticky annoyance with every other step.

I'm thinking about last night's talk with Nan.
She asked about green grass, tall trees, and rows of corn.
"No, don't see much of that around here," I said.
"Such a pity," she sighed.
But there are cabs and buses and honking horns and bikes and people,
street musicians, outdoor cafes, rumbling trucks, and people.
"Don't ever want to see any of that around here," she said.
I can't imagine a life without all of it.
"What has city life done to you?" she worried.

The crosswalk flashes an orange hand: do not cross.
The vehicles go.
The people stop.
There are coffee sippers and paper readers and cell-phone talkers.
I'm just an observer.

Tomorrow, I'm going to tell Nan
there's not much for an observer to do
in a place without people.

Base your answers to questions 16 through 18 on the poem "Something to See."

16. According to the narrator, the tall buildings on both sides of the street

     O F.   should be torn down so trees can be planted.
     O G.   block the sunlight.
     O H.   keep people moving in the right direction.
     O I.   are made of glass and brick.

17. Why is Nan worried about the narrator?

     O A.   She worries because the narrator doesn't want to live anywhere but the city.
     O B.   She worries because the narrator doesn't want to live in the city anymore.
     O C.   She worries because the narrator doesn't like walking along the crowded streets.
     O D.   She worries because the narrator doesn't want to visit her.

18. Why does the narrator carefully navigate the city's streets?

     O F.   She doesn't want to run into someone.
     O G.   She doesn't want to step on a wad of gum.
     O H.   She doesn't want to walk into oncoming traffic.
     O I.   She doesn't want to step on pieces of trash.

Read the story "Sheba" before answering questions 19 and 20.

Sheba

Growing up, my brother and I used to play in the woods behind our house. Sometimes we would play hide-and-seek with other children in the neighborhood. My favorite hiding spot took me to an overturned oak tree. The trunk had cracked close to its base. The large oak had taken down a neighboring oak with its fall. Mangled together, the fallen trunks and branch-filled tops had made a child-sized shelter. I would nestle below the natural roof, pulling my knees to my chest and keeping a careful watch for the seeker. We played many rounds of hide-and-seek before that special place was discovered.

Other times, we would just wander around by ourselves. We found all sorts of activities to amuse ourselves. One of my earliest memories was standing with my brother and trying to dig up a large rock embedded in the soil. We tried to free the boulder-like fixture with crude tools, sticks, and smaller rocks. Needless to say, we were unsuccessful. Despite its simplicity, the activity was enjoyable. That was the kind of magic held by our private forest.

As I look back on the woods, I am fondly reminded of another joy it held for my family. A hot and hazy August afternoon found us brothers seeking out snakes and turtles near the trickling stream that ran through the middle of the woods. Nothing cold-blooded was to be found that day; instead, an ugly puppy greeted us. The little dog cowered in my special hiding spot. I reached out my hand, and she crawled out to say hello. It was as if we were old friends. She was friendly and gentle, but these seemed to be her only redeeming qualities. Her dark black fur was muddy and matted, and she was unrecognizable as any particular type of dog. We were surprised to see her but happy to have her as our companion.

Sheba followed us to our house that day, and after convincing Mom, we told the dog she was home. Sheba has been a loyal member of our family since I was seven. I am still grateful that she hid in my spot until I was able to find her. She is one of the many natural wonders the woods held for us kids.

Base your answers to questions 19 and 20 on the story "Sheba."

19. Which of the following BEST describes how the narrator feels about the woods?

    ○ A. scared
    ○ B. angry
    ○ C. excited
    ○ D. fond

20. How did the narrator discover Sheba?

    ○ F. The narrator was looking for a turtle along the stream and he saw Sheba standing in the water.
    ○ G. Sheba hid in the narrator's favorite hiding spot and he found the dog.
    ○ H. The narrator's brother found Sheba and brought her to the narrator's hiding spot.
    ○ I. Sheba found the narrator in his favorite hiding spot.

Reading Practice Assessment Test

Directions for Taking the Reading Assessment Test

This assessment test contains 7 passages and 40 questions. Some of the passages are fiction, others are nonfiction. Read each passage and the questions that follow carefully. You may look back at any passage as many times as you would like. If you are unsure of a question, you can move to the next question and go back to the question you skipped later.

This test contains 40 multiple-choice questions. Multiple-choice questions require you to select the best answer possible from four choices. Only one answer is correct. Fill in the answer bubble to mark your selection.

Go On ▶

Read the excerpt from *A Connecticut Yankee in King Arthur's Court* before answering questions 1 through 6.

The following passage is an excerpt from Chapter One, titled "Camelot," of the novel *A Connecticut Yankee in King Arthur's Court*, by Mark Twain.

"CAMELOT – Camelot," said I to myself. "I don't seem to remember hearing of it before. Name of the asylum[1], likely."

It was a soft, reposeful[2] summer landscape, as lovely as a dream, and as lonesome as Sunday. The air was full of the smell of flowers, and the buzzing of insects, and the twittering of birds, and there were no people, no wagons, there was no stir of life, nothing going on. The road was mainly a winding path with hoof-prints in it, and now and then a faint trace of wheels on either side in the grass – wheels that apparently had a tire as broad as one's hand.

Presently a fair slip[3] of a girl, about ten years old, with a cataract[4] of golden hair streaming down over her shoulders, came along. Around her head she wore a hoop of flame-red poppies. It was as sweet an outfit as ever I saw, what there was of it. She walked indolently[5] along, with a mind at rest, its peace reflected in her innocent face. The circus man paid no attention to her; didn't even seem to see her. And she – she was no more startled at his fantastic make-up than if she was used to his like every day of her life. She was going by as indifferently as she might have gone by a couple of cows; but when she happened to notice me, THEN there was a change! Up went her hands, and she was turned to stone; her mouth dropped open, her eyes stared wide and timorously[6], she was the picture of astonished curiosity touched with fear. And there she stood gazing, in a sort of stupefied[7] fascination, till we turned a corner of the wood and were lost to her view. That she should be startled at me instead of at the other man, was too many for me; I couldn't make head or tail of it. And that she should seem to consider me a spectacle, and totally overlook her own merits in that respect, was another puzzling thing, and a display of magnanimity[8], too, that was surprising in one so young. There was food for thought here. I moved along as one in a dream.

[1]**asylum**: hospital
[2]**reposeful**: peaceful
[3]**slip**: young, thin person
[4]**cataract**: waterfall
[5]**indolently**: lazily
[6]**timorously**: fearfully
[7]**stupefied**: amazed
[8]**magnanimity**: kindness

Go On ▶

Base your answers to questions 1 through 6 on the excerpt from *A Connecticut Yankee in King Arthur's Court*.

1. Read this sentence from the story.

   Presently a fair slip of a girl, about ten years old, with a cataract of golden hair streaming down over her shoulders, came along.

   What comparison is the narrator making in this sentence?

   ○ A. The girl was standing under a waterfall.
   ○ B. The girl's reflection was shining in a waterfall.
   ○ C. The girl's long hair was the color of a golden waterfall.
   ○ D. The girl's long hair looked like a waterfall as it fell over her shoulders.

2. As the ten-year-old girl traveled the path, she

   ○ F. was walking with a herd of cows.
   ○ G. carried a basket of flame-red poppies.
   ○ H. was startled by the sight of the narrator.
   ○ I. was scared by the circus man.

3. Which sentence BEST summarizes this excerpt?

   ○ A. A young girl and a circus man make their way along a muddy path that is crowded with wagons.
   ○ B. A man travels along a lonely path and encounters a young girl who is surprised by the man's appearance.
   ○ C. A young girl is scared by a circus man.
   ○ D. A man travels along a lonely path and makes friends with a circus man and a young girl.

Go On ▶

4. Read this sentence from the story.

   And she – she was no more startled at his fantastic make-up than if she was used to his like every day of her life.

   What message is the narrator trying to communicate?

   ○ F. The girl was used to seeing people in colorful make-up, and she wasn't surprised at the sight of the circus man.
   ○ G. The girl had never seen anyone in fantastic make-up, but she wasn't surprised by the circus man's appearance.
   ○ H. The girl's face was painted with circus make-up, so she wasn't surprised at the sight of the circus man.
   ○ I. The girl was a member of the circus, and the man with the painted face was her father.

5. What problem does the narrator face?

   ○ A. He is scared as he travels down the path.
   ○ B. He wants to join the circus, but he isn't admitted because of his plain appearance.
   ○ C. He wants to talk with the girl, but she doesn't understand what he is saying.
   ○ D. He doesn't understand why his appearance scares the young girl.

6. What causes the narrator to lose sight of the girl?

   ○ F. She runs away from him and hides.
   ○ G. She rides off in a circus wagon.
   ○ H. The narrator turns a corner, and the woods block the view.
   ○ I. The narrator rides off in a wagon.

Read the article "The Shirtwaist Strike" before answering questions 7 through 12.

The Shirtwaist Strike

In the 1890s, a new fashion, the shirtwaist, was emerging. This woman's shirt was similar to a man's shirt, but it had thinner fabric with buttons in the back and pleats in the front. During this era, most clothes were assembled as piecework. This meant parts of a garment were cut from fabric in a factory. Workers took home the different pieces and sewed them together. Workers returned to the factory to bring together all the pieces and to assemble the complete garment. Unlike most of garments of the period, the shirtwaist was made entirely in factories.

This time in American history was not particularly kind to laborers. There were no child labor laws, no minimum wage laws, and there was very little legal protection for workers. These hard-working people endured long workdays under horrible conditions for very poor pay. It wasn't uncommon for children as young as seven to be found throughout industrial factories.

On many occasions, people protested the conditions and terms of their work, but they found little support. Out of desperation, workers joined together and formed strikes, but most manufacturers were unfazed. They hired scabs, or replacement workers. In addition, the companies had the support of the law. Strikers were often arrested and jailed. The companies also used their resources to hire thugs to harass the strikers.

Despite the setbacks, the workers did not give up. In late November 1909, garment workers in shirtwaist shops began a strike. Within one week, about 30,000 people from New York City's shirtwaist shops walked off the job. The strike spread to Philadelphia by December 20th. The strike, which lasted until February 1910, did little to change the working conditions or the pay at the factories. Additionally, the companies continued to ignore the unions formed by workers. The strike came to an end as workers returned to their jobs in order to support their families.

While the shirtwaist strike was a failure in terms of its immediate impact, the strike was an important step toward recognizing garment workers' unions. Although many of the demands of the strike were not met, the cause brought to light the conditions faced by the workers. The shirtwaist strike inspired many working women to join unions. This laid the groundwork for future strikes and for stronger unions that were influential in the development of labor laws.

Base your answers to questions 7 through 12 on the article "The Shirtwaist Strike."

7.   Read this sentence from the article.

> **Out of desperation, workers joined together and formed strikes, but most manufacturers were unfazed.**

What does the word *unfazed* mean?

○ A. not concerned
○ B. not happy
○ C. not moving
○ D. not excited

Go On ▶

8. What is the primary reason the shirtwaist strike ended?

   ○ F. The strikers were tired of being arrested.
   ○ G. The strikers needed the wages.
   ○ H. The strikers were tired of being roughed up by thugs.
   ○ I. The strikers' conditions were met.

9. Which of the following is NOT a reason that workers used for striking?

   ○ A. They wanted shorter hours.
   ○ B. They wanted better pay.
   ○ C. They wanted companies to recognize unions.
   ○ D. They wanted to bring their children to work with them.

10. The information in this article could be included in

    ○ F. a collection of personal narratives about the shirtwaist strike.
    ○ G. a report about professional women.
    ○ H. a newspaper article on the inner workings of unions.
    ○ I. a research paper on early labor movements.

11. Which of the following BEST describes this type of article?

    ○ A. an informational piece on a historical event
    ○ B. a fictional story that takes place during a historic event
    ○ C. a nonfiction article about the life of the shirtwaist strike leader
    ○ D. a persuasive piece that tries to convince readers to strike against unfair labor conditions

12. Someone who reads this article will understand

    ○ F. that the shirtwaist strikers wasted their time.
    ○ G. that shirtwaists were men's garments that were made in factories.
    ○ H. that, even though the strikers seemed to gain little, the strike had long-term effects.
    ○ I. that factory workers enjoyed their terrible working conditions.

Go On ▶

Read the article "Grand Coulee Dam" before answering questions 13 through 19.

Grand Coulee Dam

In the late 1800s, the government of the United States wanted Americans to move West in order to develop the land. Members of government knew people would need good water sources, so in 1902, Congress created the United States Bureau of Reclamation. Its job was to create water storage and irrigation west of the 100th meridian. The 100th meridian is a line of longitude in the Midwest. This line, which runs north and south, is almost at the exact center of North Dakota and South Dakota.

Early in its development stages, the Bureau of Reclamation wanted to harness the potential of the Columbia River and to utilize the natural resource as an irrigation system for Washington State. The lands of the Columbia River Basin were fertile but dry. In 1917, the Grand Coulee Dam was suggested, but many years passed before anything further happened.

In 1933, Washington State allocated $377,000 to build the Grand Coulee Dam. President Franklin Delano Roosevelt then committed $63 million in federal funds, and that December, excavation began. Construction of the main dam was completed in 1941. Water pumped from Lake Roosevelt formed the reservoir behind the dam. Powerhouses and a pumping plant were started, but their completion was interrupted.

When World War II raged in the years following the main dam's completion, the northwestern United States' aluminum industry was heavily relied upon by the war efforts. Thus, electricity production became the dam's major priority. The dam's original purpose as an irrigation tool was put on hold. Instead, six generators were brought to the dam site in order to produce hydroelectric power.

The end of the war reduced the demands for electricity, and the focus once again shifted to irrigation. In 1946, construction on the pumping plant started up again. By 1951, six pumps were in operation. Since that time, true to American ingenuity, the dam has changed with technological advances. In 1973, two pump-generators were installed. These pumps had a dual purpose. They

Go On ▶

could be used for irrigation or to generate electricity, whereas the older equipment was only available for one of these functions. By 1983, there were four more pump-generators. During periods when high amounts of electricity are required, the pumps act as generators. When the electric demands are low, the pumps are used for irrigation. The dam can irrigate up to one million acres of farmland in the Columbia River Basin.

In addition to its power pump-generators, the Grand Coulee Dam is equipped with mechanisms which enable the Bureau to regulate the rate of the river's flow. This helps the Bureau control flooding in the area.

Base your answers to questions 13 through 17 on the article "Grand Coulee Dam."

13. Why were irrigation pumps completed after electric generators?

   ○ A. Farmers would not move to an area without electricity.
   ○ B. People needed the electricity from the generators in order to build the pumps.
   ○ C. It was much easier to build the generators, so they were built first.
   ○ D. At the time, the most important need was electricity, not irrigation.

14. What did Congress intend for the Bureau of Reclamation to do?

   ○ F. to create water storage and irrigation in the western part of the country
   ○ G. to force people to settle in the west
   ○ H. to provide electricity for the western part of the country
   ○ I. to reclaim territories the government purchased from other nations

15. Read this sentence from the article.

   Since that time, true to American ingenuity, the dam has changed with technological advances.

   What is the best definition for *American ingenuity* as it is used in this article?

   ○ A. an interest in technology that replaces all old technology
   ○ B. an ability to build brand new things when they are needed
   ○ C. an ability to solve problems by looking at things from different angles
   ○ D. a group of highly educated Americans dedicated to building dams

Go On ▶

16. What is the purpose of this article?

   ○ F. to describe the original purpose of the Grand Coulee Dam
   ○ G. to explain why the Grand Coulee Dam was built as well as the dam's functions
   ○ H. to describe the importance of dams in the northwestern United States
   ○ I.   to explain how the Grand Coulee Dam was built as well as the dam's purposes

17. Which of the following is NOT a function of the Grand Coulee Dam as mentioned in this article?

   ○ A. to create electricity
   ○ B. to provide outdoor recreation
   ○ C. to provide irrigation
   ○ D. to control water flow

18. Why does the United States Bureau of Reclamation prefer pump-generators over the older equipment of the 1940s and 1950s?

   ○ F. The older equipment breaks too easily, but the pump-generators are of better quality.
   ○ G. The older equipment had only one function, but the pump-generators have dual functions.
   ○ H. The older equipment could not meet the electricity demands of the Columbia River basin, but the pump-generators are able to meet the requirements.
   ○ I.   The equipment installed in the 1940s can only be used to generate electricity, but the Bureau needed pump-generators, which are used solely for irrigation.

19. What is the main idea of the first paragraph?

   ○ A. People wanted to move west but couldn't because there was no electricity.
   ○ B. Members of government knew people would need good water sources.
   ○ C. Congress wanted to encourage settlement in the West and created the United States Bureau of Reclamation.
   ○ D. The 100th meridian is a line of longitude in the Midwest.

Go On ▶

Read the story "The Secret Share" before answering questions 20 through 26.

The Secret Share

Aishe waited in line to pay for the small paint set, the paintbrush, and the art pad. The thin, delicate hairs of the paintbrush felt like soft feathers in her hand.

"Gift wrap?" asked the sales clerk behind the counter.

"Yes," Aishe replied, scanning the selection. "Please use that silver paper, and tie it with a blue ribbon."

She watched the clerk carefully wrap each item and place it in a white box. The clerk tore a sheet of the glossy, silver paper from a large roll. She lined up the box with the paper's center, and efficiently turned the boring white box into a spectacular silver cube. Leaning her arms on the counter, Aishe selected one of the small gift cards that said Arno's Art Shop. On the inside of the card, she wrote, "See the world through the eyes of an artist. Your friend, Aishe." She tucked the little card under the cube's blue ribbon.

The day before summer vacation, Aishe carried the silver package to school. She was proud of her presentation, and she held it carefully in her hands. She didn't want anything to disturb the perfect mirror created on each side of the cube. Sunlight hit the package and reflections danced about Aishe's face. Aishe admired the gift with such adoration, if people were to look at her, they hardly would have believed she would willingly give it up. But they didn't know she had bought this gift for someone. This gift had a purpose.

Mrs. Thurston was hosting a secret-share party for her seventh-grade social studies class. It was tradition; every year, Mrs. Thurston celebrated the close of the school year with this unique festivity. Each student was assigned a partner, but Mrs. Thurston didn't want the seventh graders to reveal their partners, so the list was a secret until the last minute, when it was time for students to exchange gifts at the class party.

"Mrs. Thurston is the best," said Aishe's best friend Sunil. "I'm really going to miss her next year." The girls walked together toward the cafeteria. The halls were louder than normal. They buzzed with sounds of eager students. "She is so interested in history and in people who lived in the past . . ."

". . . but she also pays attention to people who are alive today, like us," finished Aishe.

Aishe felt certain that Mrs. Thurston would pair best friends together. At the secret-share party, Aishe would be able to exchange gifts with Sunil. Unwrapping the new supplies, Sunil might begin to enjoy art, instead of always laughing at it. On weekends, Sunil liked to say, "Come on, put away those paints, Aishe. Paint is boring and messy. Wouldn't you rather play softball?"

After Wednesday's lunch, the hall once again filled with the noise of clanging lockers. Before the bell rang, students returned to the classroom with packages. Parcels sat on each desk. The size and shape of each was as varied as the presenters. Aishe glanced with annoyance at the girl beside her, the new student named Britte. As usual, the girl sat in silence at her desk. She had wrapped her parcel in brown paper. Aishe could see that Britte had cut a brown grocery bag to fit the size of the gift. Brown tape sealed the edges together.

Go On ▶

"Boring brown paper to match Britte's boring personality," whispered a voice in the second row. Aishe could hear a ripple of giggling along the row.

"It's probably an empty box," whispered another voice behind Aishe. "A gift of nothing from the girl with nothing to say." The giggling was louder now.

Aishe wondered who would get stuck with Britte's brown package. Maybe the teacher would be Britte's secret partner; no one else wanted to be the new girl's friend.

Mrs. Thurston handed a piece of paper to a student in the front row.

"Class, this is our secret-share list," announced Mrs. Thurston. "Please find your name on the list. Your partner's name is listed beside yours. When the bell rings, pass your gift along to your partner."

With excitement, students passed the list from desk to desk. When it reached Britte, the new girl looked over at Aishe. Her eyes were shining. When Aishe saw the list, she knew why: Aishe and Britte were partners. "Oh no," Aishe grumbled inside.

Aishe felt her face grow hot. She wanted to shout, "This isn't fair. I bought this for Sunil." She wanted to run out of the room. She wanted to hide her perfect cube. But she didn't do any of those things.

The bell rang. Slowly, without raising her eyes from the desk, she handed her beautiful silver package to the new girl. Britte slid the big, ugly brown paper bag across Aishe's desk. She looked at its crude construction. Even the tape was ugly. Resentfully, she opened the boring gift from boring Britte.

Inside the brown paper, she found an inner package. It was wrapped in bright pink paper and was tied with a silver ribbon. Carefully, Aishe unwrapped the surprise. Inside, a card lay on top of a small box of . . . art supplies.

Cobalt Blue. Carmine Red. Burnt Sienna. The names of the colors seemed to glisten on the labels. Aishe read the card.

"Dear Classmate, I have loved painting ever since I was a little girl. I hope you enjoy these supplies as much as I enjoyed carefully selecting them. If you would like, I would be happy to show you how to mix these tubes of color. Painting is a wonderful hobby, and I'm sure you're really going to enjoy it. Sincerely, your new classmate, Britte."

Aishe held her breath. Turning toward the new girl, Aishe watched Britte unwrap the silver paper and open her gift.

Go On ▶

Base your answers to questions 20 through 26 on the story "The Secret Share."

20. What problem does Aishe face in this story?

　　○ F.　She doesn't know what type of gift to buy for the secret-share party.
　　○ G.　Aishe's friend, Sunil, refuses to paint portraits with Aishe.
　　○ H.　Aishe's friend, Sunil, doesn't like the art supplies Aishe bought for her.
　　○ I.　Aishe's partner for the gift exchange is Britte, a new girl she doesn't like.

21. How does the author let you know Aishe and Britte might become friends?

　　○ A.　Britte tells Aishe she wants to be her friend.
　　○ B.　They both enjoy art.
　　○ C.　They were happy to have each other as partners for the exchange.
　　○ D.　Aishe says she will be Britte's friend.

22. Did Aishe look forward to the secret-share party?

　　○ F.　Yes, she thought she would exchange gifts were her friend, Sunil.
　　○ G.　Yes, she thought Sunil would give her a nice gift.
　　○ H.　No, she did not think Sunil would be her secret-share partner.
　　○ I.　No, she did not think Sunil would enjoy her gift.

23. If this story was told from Britte's point of view, what do you think the title would be?

　　○ A.　Painting is My Favorite Hobby
　　○ B.　The Lonely Secret-Share Party
　　○ C.　A Gift I Want to Share
　　○ D.　The Ugly Gift

Go On ▶

24. Which of the following comparisons was made by one of Aishe's classmates?

    ○ F. Britte's clothes are compared to the ugly paper bag.

    ○ G. Britte's personality is compared to a boring paper bag.

    ○ H. Britte's hair is compared to the color of the paper bag.

    ○ I. Britte is compared to another new student no one likes.

25. The author of this story is MOST LIKELY trying to communicate what message?

    ○ A. Seventh-grade students can be cruel.

    ○ B. Many people enjoy painting

    ○ C. Don't judge a book by its cover.

    ○ D. Art supplies are expensive.

26. What detail does the author include that lets the reader know there may be more to Britte than Aishe realizes?

    ○ F. Britte wraps her package in a brown paper bag.

    ○ G. Britte doesn't talk with other members of the seventh-grade social studies class.

    ○ H. Aishe laughs when the other students make fun of Britte.

    ○ I. Aishe finds a brightly colored package underneath the brown paper wrapping.

Go On ▶

Read the article "Aurora Borealis: Nature's Light Show" before answering questions

Aurora Borealis: Nature's Light Show

Did you know that one of the best shows in the Northern Hemisphere isn't on TV or at the movies—it's in the sky? This phenomenon, called aurora borealis, is more commonly known as the northern lights. These lights occur in a ring around the North Pole which stretches over parts of Alaska and Canada. In the Southern Hemisphere, the lights produced are called aurora australis. Aurora polaris, which means polar lights, can be used for both the northern and southern lights.

The aurora borealis is caused by particles blown toward the Earth by solar winds. The Sun gives off high-energy charged particles. These particles, also known as ions, travel into space at speeds of 200 to 440 miles per second. The particles carry an electrical charge which interacts with the magnetic field surrounding the Earth. When these particles hit the magnetic rings around the North and South Poles, they fall into the Earth's upper atmosphere. On the way down, they run into oxygen and nitrogen to produce brilliant waves of color. The colors of the lights, which can be blues, violets, greens, and reds, depend on what the particles run into and at what height.

The solar winds blow particles from the Sun at nearly one million miles per hour, so when the particles reach the Earth, they are in constant motion. This is part of the reason why the lights appear in curtain-like waves. Another reason is that the charged particles can make the Earth's magnetic field bend and change shape. These changes can cause the spirals and other round shapes that are often seen as part of the auroras.

Although people have reported seeing the aurora borealis reach down into clouds and mountains, the lowest edge is usually between 40 and 60 miles above the Earth—much higher than any mountains, clouds, or even airplanes. The only people to fly through the aurora are astronauts, whose space shuttles fly at 190 miles above the Earth. Auroras can be more than 1,000 miles in length, but they are only about a mile wide.

Scientists have learned more about the auroras in the past half a century than they have at any other time, but they still do not know what causes some of the shapes people see in the lights. People have reported seeing shapes that resemble animals in addition to the normal thin waves. Sounds accompanying the lights have also been reported, even though the air in the atmosphere where the lights are seen is too thin to carry any sound.

Go On ▶

Before scientists discovered the cause of the lights, the various colors and shapes in the aurora borealis led to a number of myths. Some Canadian Eskimos believed the lights were torches, lighting a path to heaven. Other cultures, especially some in Europe who only saw the lights occasionally, thought they were omens of disaster.

Usually, the aurora borealis can only be seen by those close to the North Pole, but sometimes the ring stretches to cover parts of Europe and the continental United States. This happens in years when the Sun is very active. When the Sun is active, it can send huge gusts of solar wind toward the Earth, causing spectacular displays in the northern lights that can be seen much farther south than usual.

Auroras are most common during the spring and fall, although they can happen any time of year. Auroras can only be seen on clear nights, and the best time to see them is between midnight and two in the morning. Scientists can now predict when they think auroras will be visible, so in the future, many more people may have the opportunity to see these brilliant displays of light.

Base your answers to questions 27 through 31 on the article "Aurora Borealis: Nature's Light Show."

27. Read this sentence from the article.

    Other cultures, especially some in Europe who only saw the lights occasionally, thought they were omens of disaster.

    What is the meaning of the word *omen*?

    ○ A. a good luck charm
    ○ B. a sign
    ○ C. a written warning
    ○ D. a naturally occurring phenomenon

28. Which of the following is NOT a reason the lights of the aurora borealis appear in waves?

    ○ F. The particles which make up the aurora borealis are in constant motion.
    ○ G. The solar winds blow particles from the Sun at nearly one million miles per hour.
    ○ H. The light appears to move in waves, but this movement is actually an optical illusion.
    ○ I. The particles can make the Earth's magnetic field bend and change shape.

Go On ▶

29. Why did Canadian Eskimos and early European cultures develop myths about the aurora borealis?

○ A. The myths were a way for them to explain the brilliant waves of color in the sky.
○ B. The myths explained why bad things happened after seeing the lights.
○ C. The myths were a scientific explanation for the aurora borealis.
○ D. They were used to seeing the aurora borealis, and they liked to tell stories about the colors in the sky.

30. Why will most people never fly through an aurora borealis?

○ F. The aurora borealis moves too fast, and an airplane would never be able to catch it.
○ G. The aurora borealis is only an optical illusion; there is nothing for an airplane to fly through.
○ H. The lowest edge of the aurora borealis is too far above the Earth to be reached in an airplane.
○ I. The aurora borealis is too small for an airplane to pass through it.

31. What is the main idea of the seventh paragraph?

○ A. The aurora borealis is most often seen near the North Pole, but this isn't the only place it occurs.
○ B. The aurora borealis stretches south when the solar winds are active.
○ C. Only those close to the North Pole can see the aurora borealis.
○ D. The spectacular displays in the northern lights can be seen very far south of the North Pole.

©2002 Englefield & Associates, Inc.

Read the story "Super Sam" before answering questions 32 through 36.

Super Sam

"Lizzie! Lizzie! I'm Superhero! Watch me fly!"

My little brother, Sam, goes through phases. Last month, he was in a "pretending to be an animal" phase. He wanted our mom to put his dinner plate on the floor so he could eat like a dog, but she refused. Now, he's moved on to a superhero phase, and he wears this silly red cape all the time. I think it used to be part of a Halloween costume.

"Not right now, Sam," I told him, waving him away without looking up from my math book. "I have homework to finish."

"Please, Lizzie? Just watch me once," he begged. "Then I'll go away." He began to run back and forth across my bedroom, arms stretched out to the sides.

"No, Sam! Not now." I must have been talking louder than I thought, because he took a step backward. I lowered my voice. "I don't have time for your new persona[1]. I have to finish my math so I can go set the table. You know if the table isn't set when Mom gets home, she'll be mad." Sam didn't say anything, but I could tell he was trying to stomp extra hard as he left my room.

I looked at my clock after Sam left. Five o'clock. Mom would be home in fifteen minutes, and I had gotten only a few math problems done. Math was my worst subject, and I was supposed to finish it first so Mom or Dad could check it after dinner. But today's homework was much more difficult than our usual assignments, and I was nowhere near finished.

Five minutes later, I was still stuck on the problem I had been working on when Sam had interrupted me. I put my pencil down and sighed, wondering how I would be able to finish everything in time. Just as I was picking up the pencil again, I heard a crashing noise coming from downstairs.

Thoughts raced through my mind as I ran down the stairs. My first thought was that Sam had probably knocked over something while he was running around, pretending to fly. But what if it was something else? What if someone had broken into our house? What if Sam was hurt?

"Sam?" I called his name as I looked in the front hallway, then in the living room. I was about to move on to the dining room when I heard someone whimpering quietly. The sound seemed to be coming from the kitchen. I peeked my head through the doorway. Sam was on top of the counter, huddled beneath the cabinets. There was a broken plate on the floor.

I approached the edge of the counter. "Sam?" I asked gently, "What happened?"

Go On ▶

Sam raised his head. "I was going to set the table," he said, sniffling, "but I couldn't reach the plates. So, I got up here. I dropped it when I tried to climb down."

The plate had broken into six or seven big pieces. I picked them up and put them in the trash can. Then I walked back over to the counter and put my hand on top of Sam's. I couldn't help noticing how small it was.

"Why were you trying to set the table, Sam? You know that's my job."

Sam looked up at me with big round eyes. "But you were working so hard, and I didn't want you to get in trouble. Besides," he said, his eyes becoming brighter, "Superhero can set the table with lightning speed!"

I laughed and pulled him down from the countertop. "Tell you what, Superhero. How about if we set the table together? I'll get the plates and glasses, and you can do the silverware."

"Well . . ." he said doubtfully, "I guess Superhero could do the silverware."

"And after that," I said, "maybe you can fly for me." Sam's face lit up. He opened the drawer and started pulling out silverware as fast as he could. I smiled as he hurried to the table, his cape flapping behind him. Sometimes, he was a lot more super than I gave him credit for.

¹**persona**: identity

Base your answers to questions 32 through 36 on the story "Super Sam."

32. Read this sentence from the story.

> **I don't have time for your new persona.**

Why does Lizzie feel this way?

○ F. She is busy and doesn't want to be bothered by her little brother's latest phase.
○ G. She wants her brother to set the table so she doesn't have to do it.
○ H. She wants her brother to help her with her homework instead of acting like Superhero.
○ I. She is tired of her brother's phases, and she wants him to act like a normal kid.

Go On ▶

33. What causes Lizzie to decide to play along with Sam's Superhero character?

   ○ A. Sam breaks a plate and she wants him to clean it up.
   ○ B. Sam tries to give Lizzie time to do her homework by attempting to set the table.
   ○ C. Sam tells Lizzie he will set the silverware if she watches him fly.
   ○ D. Sam won't stop crying until Lizzie plays along.

34. Which of the following describes Lizzie?

   ○ F. attentive and happy
   ○ G. carefree and kind
   ○ H. angry and upset
   ○ I. annoyed but caring

35. What problem does Lizzie encounter early in the story?

   ○ A. She has trouble with her math homework.
   ○ B. Sam drops a plate.
   ○ C. Sam won't set the table.
   ○ D. Sam won't stop acting like a dog.

36. Why did the author write this story?

   ○ F. to entertain readers
   ○ G. to explain why children act like superheroes
   ○ H. to tell the story of an unhappy little boy
   ○ I. to persuade readers to talk with their siblings

Go On ▶

Read "Clean Machines" and "Mix and Match" before answering questions 37 through 40.

Clean Machines

Lift the hood of 99.99% of the automobiles on the road today, and you will find an internal combustion engine. This engine depends on irreplaceable fossil fuels and creates emissions that pollute. Emissions contribute to the depletion[1] of the ozone layer and to the greenhouse effect. As more and more cars are demanded around the world, the environmental effects are bound to expand.

Enter California. Ninety-five percent of Californians live in areas that do not meet federally required clean air standards because of a high amount of emissions. Most people blame the conditions on cars and trucks. Based on these dismal figures, legislators decided to act. By 2003, 10% of cars sold in California must be non-polluting. Other states, including New York and Massachusetts, have instituted similar regulations, forcing auto manufacturers to act.

Electric cars are the most obvious answer to the nonpolluting, non-emissions standard. Since the fuel crisis of the 1970s, auto manufacturers have increased their experiments with battery powered cars; however, these have many drawbacks. After less than 100 miles, the batteries must be recharged, which can take as long as eight hours. The batteries are very heavy; they can double the weight of the car. Finally, they are extremely expensive and need to be replaced every three to four years. All these factors have contributed to the belief that battery-driven electric cars are not very practical.

However, new technology on the horizon will hopefully make electric cars more appealing. The answer to the battery problem appears to be the fuel cell. A fuel cell is not a battery that stores an electrical charge. Instead, it creates electricity on the move using hydrogen, with the only byproduct being water. Thus, it does not need to be plugged in to recharge and is lighter than traditional batteries.

Fuel cell technology has been improved and it may be an option, but the fuel itself presents a problem. Gasoline and methanol[2] are the fuels of choice right now, since the technology for using hydrogen is still primitive. The gasoline or methanol is refined in an on-board processor to extract hydrogen. This method still creates some emissions, but not nearly the amount created by a traditional internal combustion engine. Problems: gasoline is the fossil fuel we are trying to avoid using in the first place, and methanol is highly toxic. Also, the process to change gasoline or methanol to hydrogen is difficult. Using pure hydrogen is the best alternative, since the only emissions it would create would be water and heat; however, it is difficult to compress[3] enough hydrogen to make the car go very far, and hydrogen is extremely flammable. Researchers are working on the technology, but until they come up with a safe and efficient method, gasoline and methanol appear to be the only options.

Independent carmakers are rushing to develop the best technology for electric cars. Amory Lovins of the Rocky Mountain Institute is working on a car made completely of plastics. Major auto manufacturers are also dedicating teams of engineers to working on fuel cell cars. They see this as the car of the future, with no dependence on fossil fuels and no emissions to contribute to the greenhouse effect—in short, a car with no negative environmental impact whatsoever.

Go On ▶

Mix and Match

Carmakers and consumers are discovering that sometimes finding the solution to a problem does not mean throwing out something altogether, but revising it. In the wake of new demands for nonpolluting automobiles, manufacturers have come up with a compromise in the form of the hybrid car.

Electric cars have appeared to be the ideal solution to the gas-guzzling, polluting cars with internal combustion engines. However, electric cars have problems, including the limited distance they can travel and the weight and expense of batteries. Hybrid cars solve these problems while also dramatically cutting down on polluting emissions.

These cars are called "hybrids" because they mix and match technology, using a combination of energy sources. They use both an internal combustion engine and a small set of batteries. The batteries are less expensive and lighter than those found in purely electric cars. Unlike older versions of electric cars, which ran on huge batteries, hybrids do not need to be plugged in to recharge. Instead, they use the excess power from the gas engine to charge the batteries.

Hybrids combine the best of both gasoline and electric-powered worlds. Gasoline engines are most efficient in driving long distances at faster speeds, but they waste a great deal of fuel, especially when the car starts and when it runs while not moving. Electric motors, on the other hand, are efficient when starting up and do not pollute while the car is standing still; however, in highway driving, their batteries run down quickly. A hybrid uses the electric motor to start the car and to accelerate. Once the car gets going, the gasoline engine kicks in. While driving, the hybrid uses the excess power from the engine to recharge the batteries.

Makers of hybrids report fuel economy of up to 70 miles per gallon, more than twice as efficient as most compact cars with internal combustion engines, which means half the emissions. Not a bad compromise.

[1]**depletion**: gradual destruction
[2]**methanol**: a liquid; made from carbon monoxide and hydrogen; used as a fuel source
[3]**compress**: to compact using pressure

Go On ▶

Base your answers to questions 37 through 40 on the articles "Clean Machines" and "Mix and Match."

37. What kind of engine do most cars have today?

    ○ A. electric
    ○ B. hybrid
    ○ C. internal combustion
    ○ D. fuel cell

38. Why are electric cars seen as the ideal replacement for the internal combustion engines?

    ○ F. They do not pollute the air.
    ○ G. They are simpler to make.
    ○ H. They are already widely available.
    ○ I. They can travel for long distances.

39. What problem does the fuel cell introduce?

    ○ A. It is extremely heavy.
    ○ B. It needs to be plugged in to be recharged.
    ○ C. The fuel that would work best is difficult to compress.
    ○ D. Its emissions are greater than the internal combustion engine.

40. In the context of these articles, what is the best definition of *hybrid*?

    ○ F. Something that gives up its good qualities for the good qualities of another.
    ○ G. Something having two kinds of components that work together to produce a common result.
    ○ H. Something that replaces another item of the same kind.
    ○ I. Something that is a pure breed.

Mathematics

Introduction

In the Mathematics section of the Florida Comprehensive Assessment Test (FCAT), you will be asked questions to test the knowledge you have learned so far in school. These questions have been written based on the mathematics you have been taught in school through seventh grade. The questions you answer are not meant to confuse or to trick you but are written so you have the best opportunity to show what you know about mathematics.

Within this section of the FCAT, you will be faced with two question types including multiple-choice and gridded-response questions. These different question types will give you many ways to demonstrate the skills you know. For an explanation on these types of questions, refer to pages vi.

This chapter covers all Mathematics Strands, Standards, and Benchmarks. Each Benchmark is addressed with a sample question. You will complete these exercises designed to help you practice your test-taking skills. Following these practice items, a full-length sample assessment test has been created to simulate the experience of taking the FCAT Mathematics test. A glossary of mathematical terms you may encounter on the FCAT is provided beginning on page 84.

Practice Items

1. Which of the following choices is the same as **192,806**?

    ○ A. one hundred ninety-two eight hundred six
    ○ B. one hundred ninety-two eight hundred six thousand
    ○ C. one hundred ninety-two thousand eight hundred sixty
    ◉ D. one hundred ninety-two thousand eight hundred six

2. Which of the following numbers is the **greatest**?

    ○ F. $\dfrac{190}{10}$

    ○ G. 20%

    ◉ H. 2.2 x 10^1

    ○ I. $\dfrac{6}{150}$

3. Marty and Jim ordered a pizza. Jim ate 3 times as much pizza as Marty did. Which of the following represents the amount of pizza Jim ate?

    ○ A. 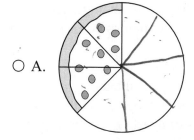   ○ C.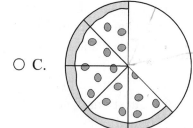

    ○ B. 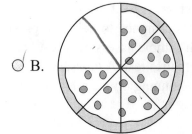   ○ D.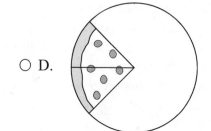

4. On the last spelling test, Hallie spelled 19 words correctly out of the 20 words on the test. What percent of the words on the spelling test did Hallie spell correctly?

○ F. 1%
○ G. 19%
○ H. 95%
○ I. 99%

5. What is the value of the following expression?

$$2.5 \times 10^2 - 5^2$$

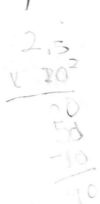

○ A. 0
○ B. 50
○ C. 100
○ D. 225

6. In the expression below, using what operation will result in the greatest number?

$$\frac{5}{12} \ \square \ \frac{5}{6}$$

○ F. subtraction
○ G. addition
○ H. division
○ I. multiplication

7. In the expression below, what operation should be performed **first**?

$$6 + 4 \times (8 - 2)$$

○ A. Add 6 and 4.
○ B. Add 8 and 4
○ C. Subtract 2 from 8.
○ D. Multiply 6 and 4

8. Theo went to his garden to pick apples from his apple tree. Of the 60 apples he counted on the tree, only 20% of them were ripe. If Theo picked only the ripe apples from the tree, how many apples did Theo pick?

   ○ F. 3 apples
   ○ G. 5 apples
   ○ H. 12 apples
   ○ I. 20 apples

9. An orange juice squeezing machine is able to squeeze the juice out of 27 oranges every minute. If one shipment of orange juice requires 2,671 oranges to be squeezed, ESTIMATE how long will it take an orange juice squeezing machine to squeeze enough oranges for one shipment of orange juice?

   ○ A. 10 minutes
   ○ B. 27 minutes
   ○ C. 57 minutes
   ○ D. 90 minutes

10. Which of the following lists of numbers includes **only** prime numbers?

   ○ F. 1, 2, 5, 7, 23
   ○ G. 3, 4, 7, 11, 29
   ○ H. 5, 11, 21, 31, 41
   ○ I. 2, 13, 19, 23, 29

11. The pentagon shown below is a regular pentagon. Triangle PNT has an area of 630. The distance between Point P and NT is 45. This distance is also the height of Triangle PNT. Using this information, what is the perimeter of Pentagon PENTA?

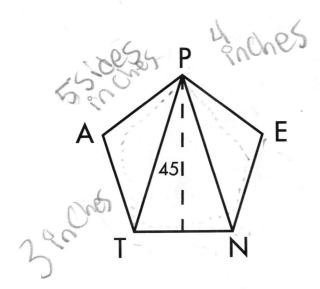

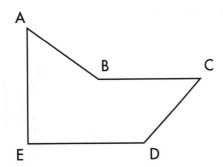

12. At which point in the figure below is an **obtuse** angle located?

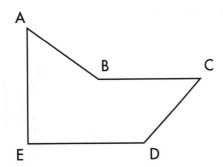

   ○ A. Point A
   ○ B. Point C
   ○ C. Point D
   ○ D. Point E

13. Diego is painting a mural to hang in his room. The mural is painted on a rectangular canvas that measures 2 feet long by 3 feet wide. When the mural is complete, Diego frames the mural with a frame that is 2 inches thick. How much greater is the area of the frame and mural together than the area of the mural without a frame?

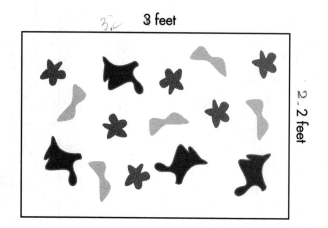

3 feet

2 2 feet

○ F. 96 square inches
○ G. 124 square inches
○ H. 144 square inches
○ I. 256 square inches

14. In the scale drawing below, the flagpole is 3 inches high. According to the scale given below, what is the actual height of the flagpole?

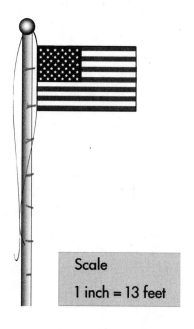

Scale

1 inch = 13 feet

15. Jimmy and his friends are having a watermelon-seed spitting contest. Jimmy was able to spit a seed 3 times as far as Gwen. Art only managed to spit a seed half as far as Kelly. Gwen's seed landed just past Kelly's seed. Order Jimmy and his friends from the person whose seed was spit the farthest to the person whose seed was spit the shortest distance.

○ A. Jimmy, Gwen, Art, Kelly
○ B. Art, Kelly, Gwen, Jimmy
○ C. Jimmy, Gwen, Kelly, Art
○ D. Jimmy, Art, Gwen Kelly

16. The length of the bobsled track at the 2002 Winter Olympics was 4,397 feet. How long was this bobsled track in **yards**?

○ F. 1,465.67 yards
○ G. 2,198.5 yards
○ H. 2,931.34 yards
○ I. 3,292.75 yards

17. Tyrone mows lawns in his neighborhood to earn extra money. He charges $0.01 per square yard of grass he mows. Mr. Chen's lawn is shown below. ESTIMATE how much money Tyrone will earn by mowing Mr. Chen's lawn.

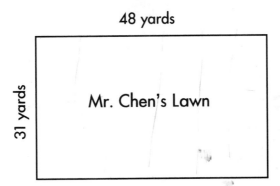

48 yards

31 yards

Mr. Chen's Lawn

○ A. $12.00
○ B. $15.00
○ C. $20.00
○ D. $30.00

18. In Quadrilateral ABCE below, Angle ABC is divided into two congruent angles by BD. Angle BCE is 60°. What is the measure of Angle ABD?

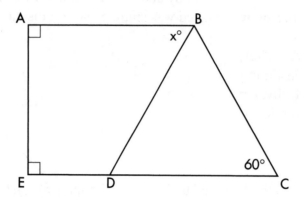

○ F. 30°
○ G. 60°
○ H. 100°
○ I.   120°

19. Look at the cheetah pictured below. Which of the following choices shows the cheetah rotated 180º?

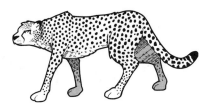

○ A.    ○ C.

○ B. 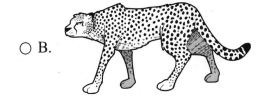   ○ D.

20. Which of the following objects could **NOT** be used to create a tessellation?

○ F.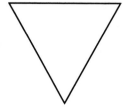

○ H.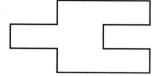

○ G.

○ I.

21. Through which of the following points can a line be drawn so that it passes through Point A **and** is perpendicular to the y-axis?

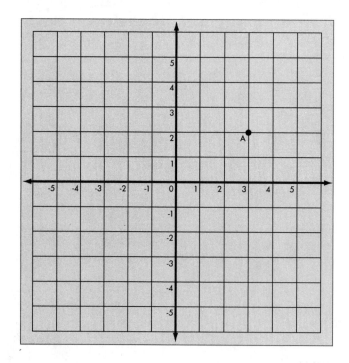

○ A. (4, 3)
○ B. (4, 2)
○ C. (2, 4)
○ D. (3, 4)

22. At what coordinate is Point S located on the grid below?

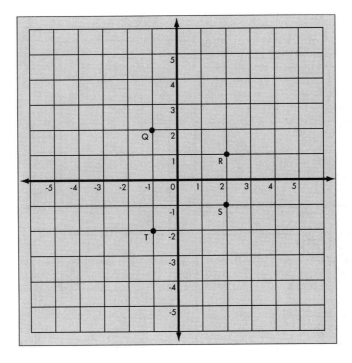

○ F. (2, -1)
○ G. (-1, -2)
○ H. (-1, 2)
○ I. (2, 1)

23. Use the function table given below to solve for *y* when *x* = 5.

x	y
1	-3
2	1
3	5
4	9
5	
6	17
7	21

©2002 Englefield & Associates, Inc.   65

24. Based on the coordinates given on the line in the graph below, what is the relationship between *x* and *y*?

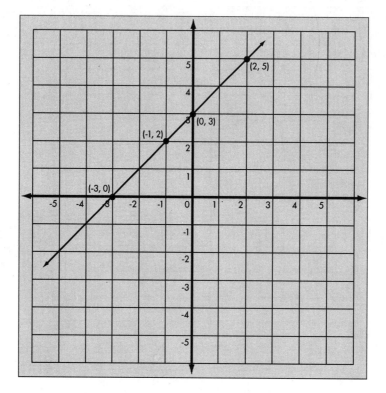

○ A. $y = x + 3$
○ B. $y = x + 1$
○ C. $y = 2x + 3$
○ D. $y = 3x + 1$

25. During a fishing trip, Kendall caught 4 fewer bass than 3 times the number of walleye (*w*) he caught. Which of the following expressions could be used to determine the number of bass Kendall caught?

○ F. $4w + 3$
○ G. $4w - 3$
○ H. $3w - 4$
○ I. $3w + 4$

26. A local bakery sells doughnuts by the dozen only. The first dozen costs $10.00. Each dozen after that costs $8.50. Mario is buying doughnuts for a fundraiser breakfast at his school. He spends a total of $163.00 on doughnuts. This information is displayed in the equation below, where *n* represents the number of dozens of doughnuts Mario purchased. According to the equation, how many dozens of doughnuts did Mario purchase?

$$\$10.00 + (n - 1)(\$8.50) = \$163.00$$

27. Three classes at Juniper Junior High School held a drive to collect canned goods for a homeless shelter. According to the graph below, which of the following is **true**?

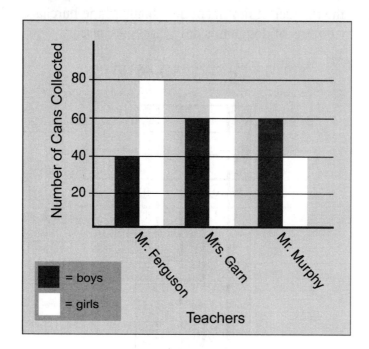

- ○ A. Mr. Ferguson's class collected the most cans.
- ○ B. In Mr. Murphy's class, the girls collected 20 more cans than the boys.
- ○ C. In each class, the girls collected more cans than the boys.
- ○ D. Overall, the girls collected more cans than the boys.

28. The starting roster for the Perrysburg Dragons baseball team is given below. What is the **mean** number of letters in the players' last names?

Pos.	No.	First Name	Last Name
CF	14	Dean	Coughlan
2B	9	Javier	Rodriguez
LF	3	Wade	Sullivant
1B	11	Rusty	Johnson
RF	5	Franco	Youmans
3B	10	Andre	Stetson
SS	17	Kyle	Silverburg
C	2	Trevor	Castillo
P	19	Roger	Hubbell

○ F. 5
○ G. 7
○ H. 8
○ I. 10

29. Mrs. Wilshire's science class was observing ladybugs. They collected 11 ladybugs and counted the number of spots each ladybug had. Then, they recorded this information in the graph below. According to the data recorded in the graph, which of the following values will be the **lowest** for this data?

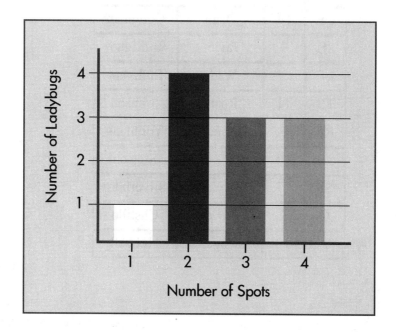

- ○ A. the mean number of spots
- ○ B. the median number of spots
- ○ C. the mode of the number of spots
- ○ D. the range of the number of spots

30. Abe flipped a penny 5 times. Each time, it landed on "heads." Which of the following statements is **true**?

- ○ F. The next time Abe flips the penny, it will most likely land on "heads."
- ○ G. The next time Abe flips the penny, it will most likely land on "tails."
- ○ H. The penny will most likely land on "tails" the next 5 times it is flipped.
- ○ I. The next time Abe flips the penny, it has an equal chance of landing on "heads" or "tails."

31. Stephanie wanted a puppy. At the pet store, she saw 6 golden retrievers, 3 beagles, 2 basset hounds, and 1 springer spaniel. What is the probability that Stephanie chose a beagle?

   ○ A. $\dfrac{1}{3}$

   ○ B. $\dfrac{1}{4}$

   ○ C. $\dfrac{1}{6}$

   ○ D. $\dfrac{1}{12}$

32. At Marcia's Candy Emporium, each worker's candy production is closely watched and recorded. During one week, Michael produced twice his normal number of chocolates. Michael produced 100 boxes of chocolate, although his mean production was 50 boxes of chocolate. Which of the following predictions could you make from this information?

   ○ F. Michael's chocolate production will continue to increase.
   ○ G. Michael's chocolate production will return to normal eventually.
   ○ H. The chocolate production of the other workers will increase.
   ○ I. The chocolate production of the other workers will decrease.

33. Sandler Elementary School was planning on adding a new item to its lunch menu. The cafeteria workers decided to ask the students what they thought should be added to the menu. A poll was taken during each lunch hour of students standing in the line to buy their lunches. The item receiving the most votes was fettuccine alfredo. What error was made during the data collection poll?

   ○ A. The poll should only have been given to 6th graders because they have been at the school longer and know what is better.
   ○ B. The poll should not have been limited to people buying their lunches.
   ○ C. The poll should not have been given to students because they would most likely choose something unhealthy.
   ○ D. The poll should have included choices for the students because they probably do not have any good ideas.

Mathematics Practice Assessment Test

Directions for Taking the Mathematics Assessment Test

On this section of the Florida Comprehensive Assessment Test (FCAT), you will answer 40 questions. For multiple-choice questions, you will be asked to pick the best answer out of four possible choices. Fill in the answer bubble to mark your selection. On gridded-response questions, each question requires a numerical answer which should be filled into a five-column number grid.

Read each question carefully and answer it to the best of your ability. If you do not know an answer, you may skip the question and come back to it later.

Figures and diagrams with given lengths and/or dimensions are NOT drawn to scale. Angle measures should be assumed to be accurate. Use the formula sheet on page 105 and the conversion table on page 99 to help you answer the questions. You will also be given a calculator to use.

When you finish, check your answers.

1. The Statue of Liberty weighs 450,000 pounds. How many **tons** does the Statue of Liberty weigh?

    ○ A. 45 tons
    ○ B. 225 tons
    ○ C. 281 tons
    ○ D. 450 tons

2. Pete and Becca own a llama farm. On their farm, they have 240 llamas. Each llama they sell earns them $325.00 profit. If they were to sell 60% of their llamas, how much total profit would they make?

    ○ F. $31,200.00
    ○ G. $46,800.00
    ○ H. $62,400.00
    ○ I. $78,000.00

3. The sales figures from 2000 for Wizard Productions are shown in the circle graph below. The sales from videos accounted for 10% of the total sales and brought in $3,600,000.00. Use this information to determine the total amount of sales resulting from books in 2000.

    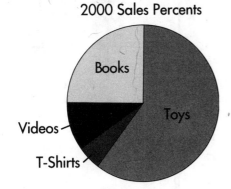
    2000 Sales Percents

    ○ A. $7,200,000.00
    ○ B. $9,000,000.00
    ○ C. $14,400,000.00
    ○ D. $16,200,000.00

4. Look at the expression given below and determine what should be done **first**?

    $$(3^2 - 4) \times 2 + 8$$

    ○ F. Subtract 4 from 3.
    ○ G. Add 2 and 8.
    ○ H. Multiply 4 by 2.
    ○ I. Multiply 3 by 3.

5. Which of the following pairs of lines are **parallel** to one another?

    ○ A.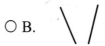
    ○ B.
    ○ C.
    ○ D.

Go On ▶
Go On ▶

6. What is the sum of the interior angles of a stop sign? Your answer will be in **degrees**.

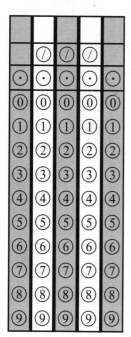

7. Which of the following is **NOT** true about the line $y = 3$?

   ○ F.   It is parallel to the y-axis.
   ○ G.   It passes through (2, 3).
   ○ H.   It does not pass through (3, 4).
   ○ I.   It never crosses the x-axis.

8. Robin was competing in an archery tournament. On the previous three arrows she shot, she had scored 7, 0, and 3 points respectively. Her total for this round of the tournament is 17 points so far. If she has one more arrow to shoot, which of the following expressions **best** represents what her final point total (p) for the round could be?

   ○ A. $p > 17$
   ○ B. $p < 17$
   ○ C. $p = 17$
   ○ D. $p \geq 17$

9. Jay invited some of his friends over to his house for a slumber party. During the party, they ordered pizza. The graph below shows how many people ate certain numbers of pieces of pizza. Use the graph to determine the **mode** of the number of pieces of pizza eaten by Jay and his friends.

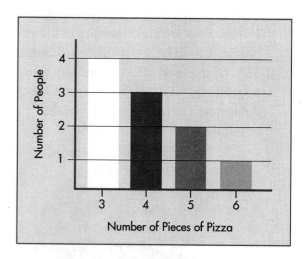

   ○ F.   3 pieces
   ○ G.   4 pieces
   ○ H.   5 pieces
   ○ I.   6 pieces

Go On ▶   Go On ▶

74   ©2002 Englefield & Associates, Inc.

10. Horatio is reading a book about sunken ships in the Mediterranean Sea. The book is 256 pages long; 64 of the pages have illustrations on them. What are the odds that Horatio will open the book to a page with a picture on it?

○ A. $\dfrac{1}{256}$

○ B. $\dfrac{1}{64}$

○ C. $\dfrac{3}{32}$

○ D. $\dfrac{1}{4}$

11. Yolanda is helping the drama club construct a set for an upcoming play. They need to construct a giant pencil. They base their design on a pencil that is 6.5 inches long. If each inch of the model pencil represents 3 feet of the giant pencil, how long will the giant pencil be?

○ F. 9.5 feet
○ G. 13.0 feet
○ H. 19.5 feet
○ I. 26.0 feet

12. In a bag of candy, there are an equal number of each of four colors: red, green, yellow, and blue. Randy randomly selects 16 pieces of candy from the bag. Of those 16 pieces of candy, 6 of the pieces of candy are red. How does this result compare with what would be expected based on probability?

○ A. The number of pieces of red candy Randy selected is greater than what would be expected.
○ B. The number of pieces of red candy Randy selected is less than what would be expected.
○ C. The number of pieces of red candy Randy selected is equal to what would be expected.
○ D. The expected probability cannot be determined without knowing the exact number of pieces of candy in the bag.

13. Kyle is helping fix playground equipment at a local park. He is responsible for increasing the size of the sandbox, shown below. To do this, he will add 2 feet to the width of the sandbox. How will the perimeter of the sandbox change if Kyle adds 2 feet to the width of the sandbox?

6 feet

4 feet

Sandbox

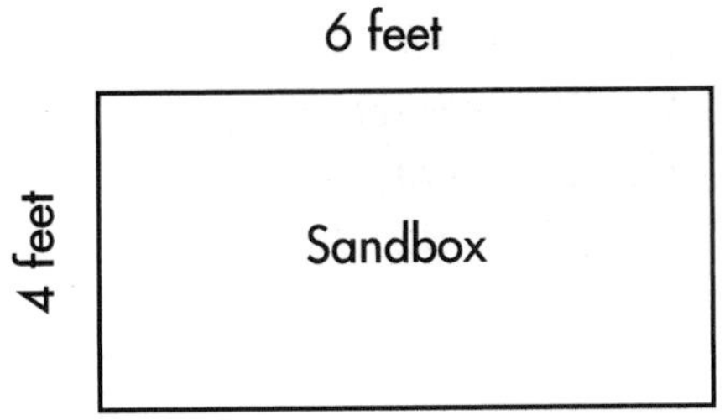

○ F. The perimeter will increase by 2 feet.
○ G. The perimeter will increase by 4 feet.
○ H. The perimeter will increase by 8 feet.
○ I. The perimeter will be twice as large.

Go On ▶

Go On ▶

14. Consuela used a grid to map out some of her favorite places in town. What is located at the point (-2, 4)?

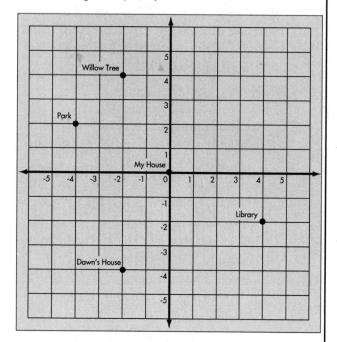

- ○ A. the park
- ○ B. the library
- ○ C. the willow tree
- ○ D. Dawn's house

15. Which of the following could also be written as **three million four hundred thousand five**?

- ○ F. 3,405,000
- ○ G. 3,040,005
- ○ H. 3,045,000
- ○ I. 3,400,005

16. Roosevelt was conducting a survey of people's favorite beverages. On two separate nights, he conducted his survey at the two most popular restaurants in Huckleberry. The results of his survey are shown in the table below. Which of the following can you determine from the information in the table?

Beverage	Restaurant	
	Spumoni's	Donata's
Soda Pop	43	35
Orange Juice	22	20
Lemonade	17	12
Water	24	19

- ○ A. The most popular restaurant in Huckleberry.
- ○ B. The total number of people who ordered lemonade at Donata's the night of the survey..
- ○ C. The number of customers Spumoni's served the night of the survey.
-   D. The percent of the total votes lemonade received.

17. The square below contains all but which of the following?

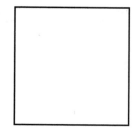

- ○ F. parallel lines
- ○ G. obtuse angles
- ○ H. congruent sides
- ○ I. perpendicular lines

Go On ▶

Go On ▶

18. Austin was building a model car. After 30 minutes, he had $\frac{7}{8}$ of the model complete. What **decimal** represents how much of the model he had completed after 30 minutes?

20. Gunner has a Frisbee with a diameter of 14 inches. What is the circumference of the Frisbee? Use 3.14 as a value for π.

21. Which of the following numbers is **NOT** a factor of 36?

○ F. 6
○ G. 12
○ H. 16
○ I. 18

19. Carrie and her friends wanted to find out who was the tallest of the 4 of them. Samantha knew she was taller than Miranda, and Carrie knew she was taller than Charlotte. After measuring, Carrie saw she was taller than Miranda, but not Samantha. If Miranda is taller than at least one of her friends, what is the order of Carrie and her friends from tallest to shortest?

○ A. Samantha, Miranda, Carrie, Charlotte
○ B. Samantha, Carrie, Miranda, Charlotte
○ C. Carrie, Samantha, Miranda, Charlotte
○ D. Carrie, Samantha, Charlotte, Miranda

Go On ▶

Go On ▶

22. Kit's dog Oliver likes to dig holes. This week, Oliver dug 19 holes in the yard. ESTIMATE the number of holes Oliver will dig in the yard over a year if he digs holes at about the same rate per week all year?

○ A. 500 holes
○ B. 1,000 holes
○ C. 1,200 holes
○ D. 1,500 holes

23. Which of the following shows the numbers in order from **least** to **greatest**?

○ F. 33%, 0.35, $\frac{3}{5}$, $\frac{2}{3}$

○ G. $\frac{2}{3}$, 33%, 0.35, $\frac{3}{5}$

○ H. $\frac{2}{3}$, $\frac{3}{5}$, 33%, 0.35,

○ I. $\frac{3}{5}$, 0.35, 33%, $\frac{2}{3}$

24. In the diagram below, what is the measure of the angle **supplemental** to Angle BAC? Your answer will be in degrees.

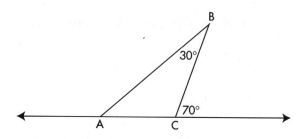

25. Gunter's mom is making mashed potatoes for Thanksgiving dinner. She asks Gunter to go to the store to get her 10 pounds of potatoes. At the store, Gunter weighs one potato and sees it weighs 4.3 ounces. If each potato weighs about the same amount, ESTIMATE the number of potatoes Gunter needs to buy.

○ A. 15 potatoes
○ B. 25 potatoes
○ C. 32 potatoes
○ D. 40 potatoes

Go On ▶

Go On ▶

26. Renae was playing a board game with some of her friends. On her next turn, she needed to roll a "3" on a regular die to win the game. The three people who went before her all rolled "3s" on their turns. Which of the following statements about Renae's next turn is true?

   ○ F. Renae will most likely roll a "3" because her friends have been able to do so.
   ○ G. Renae will most likely roll a "3" because she is trying to.
   ○ H. Renae will most likely not roll a "3" because so many "3s" have already been rolled in a row.
   ○ I. Renae has an equal chance of rolling any number on the die.

27. The results of a pie-eating contest are shown in the table below. What was the **median** number of pies eaten during the contest?

Name	Pies Eaten
Heidi	4
John	7
Summer	4
Carlos	6
Jennifer	4
J.J.	8
Monica	7

   ○ A. 4
   ○ B. 5
   ○ C. 6
   ○ D. 7

28. Which of the following will result in the **greatest** number?

   ○ F. squaring $\dfrac{2}{5}$

   ○ G. dividing $\dfrac{2}{5}$ by 2

   ○ H. subtracting $\dfrac{1}{10}$ from $\dfrac{2}{5}$

   ○ I. multiplying $\dfrac{2}{5}$ by $\dfrac{1}{10}$

29. Predrag was baking cookies for a Valentine's Day party. He baked some cookies in the shape of a heart and others in the shape of an arrow. Of the cookies he baked, 40% were shaped like arrows. Which of the cookie trays below best represents this?

   ○ A.

   ○ B.

   ○ C.

   ○ D.

Go On ▶   Go On ▶

30. At an apple orchard, a farmer charges $10.00 to pick the first bushel of apples and $3.00 for each bushel after that. Which expression could be used to find the price of picking *n* bushels of apples?

   ○ F. (*n* − 1) x ($3.00 + $10.00)
   ○ G. (*n* − 1) x $3.00 + $10.00
   ○ H. (*n* − 1) x $3.00 + $10.00 x *n*
   ○ I. *n* − 1 x $3.00 + $10.00

31. What is the value of the expression given below?

$$3^3 + 3^5 - 2^5$$

32. What is the value of *y* when *x* = 2 in the function table below?

x	y
1	0.125
2	
3	0.5
4	1
5	2
6	4
7	8

Go On ▶   **Go On** ▶

33. Which of the following figures could be used to create a tessellation?

○ A.
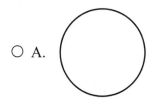

○ B.

○ C.
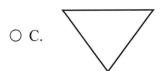

○ D.

34. Which of the following is the same as 0.150?

○ F. fifteen-tenths
○ G. fifteen-hundredths
○ H. fifteen-hundreds
○ I.   fifteen-thousandths

35. What is the measure of Angle CAD in the diagram below? Your answer will be in degrees.

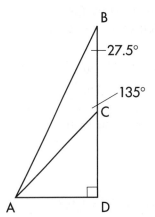

Go On ▶

Go On ▶

36. Each year, the town of Bakersville holds the Great Cake Race. Each participant runs 2.5 miles while balancing a cake on his or her head. How long is the Great Cake Race in **yards**?

    ○ A. 3,520 yards
    ○ B. 4,400 yards
    ○ C. 10,560 yards
    ○ D. 12,200 yards

37. Mr. Bohr's class is conducting a science experiment about temperature. They need to know the temperature in degrees Celsius. Mr. Bohr gave them the equation below to find the temperature in degrees Celsius if they know the temperature in degrees Fahrenheit. If it is 61° F, what is the temperature in degrees Celsius? Round your answer to the nearest tenth.

$$(°F - 32) \times \frac{5}{9} = °C$$

38. Keith and his friends were running laps during gym class. They had to see how many laps around the gym they could run in 15 minutes. According to the table below, who ran the same number of laps as the **mean** number of laps run?

Name	Laps
Keith	12
Chris	7
Eddie	11
Howard	3
Archie	9
Les	10
Vic	11

○ F. Archie
○ G. Eddie
○ H. Howard
○ I. Les

Go On ▶

Go On ▶

39. Heather is eating a box of animal crackers. In the box, there are 5 lions, 4 monkeys, 2 elephants, and 1 bear. If Heather takes an animal cracker from the box without looking, what are the odds she will choose an elephant?

○ A. $\frac{1}{12}$

○ B. $\frac{1}{6}$

○ C. $\frac{1}{3}$

○ D. $\frac{1}{2}$

40. Curtis is planning to buy a new radio. The radio he wants costs $29.99, but he has a coupon for $5.00 off. When he gets to the store, the radio is marked as 10% off. If sales tax is 6%, how much will Curtis pay for the radio? Your answer will be in dollars.

Go On ▶

Glossary of Words on the 7th Grade Mathematics FCAT

Absolute Value – The non-negative value of any number. For example, the absolute value of 4 is 4, and the absolute value of -4 is also 4. Absolute value is simply how far away a number is on a number line from the number 0. For example, on a number line, if you travel from -6 to -4, you might subtract -6 from -4 to see how far you traveled. In this case, you get -2, which is an impossible distance to travel. You must take the absolute value of -2, which shows you traveled 2 units. Absolute value is denoted by the following, where *n* is any real number: | *n* |.

Acute – An **angle** with a measure between 0° and 90°. (see example page 102)

Altitude – In a polygon, a line drawn from any vertex to any side so that the line is perpendicular to the side to which it is drawn.

Angle – The distance, recorded in degrees (°), between two **segments**, rays, or lines which meet at a common **vertex**. Angles can be **obtuse**, **acute**, **right**, or straight. A **straight angle** is a straight line, which measures 180°. (see example page 102)

Approximate – To obtain an answer that is not necessarily exact, but close enough for the given situation. An example of a situation in which approximation is appropriate would be if you were asked to figure out how many people there are in the world. It would be almost impossible to know the exact figure, but an approximate answer would give you a good idea of the answer. Another way to say you are approximating something is to **estimate** it.

Area – The amount of **two-dimensional** space enclosed by an object is referred to as its area. In its simplest form, area can be thought of as the length of the object multiplied by its width. The **units of measurement** used to express area are always some form of a square unit, such as square inches or square meters. The most common abbreviation for area is A.

Associative Property – For any numbers a, b, and c, in addition: (a + b) + c = a + (b + c); for multiplication: (a x b) x c = a x (b x c).

Average – The **sum** of a **set** of numbers divided by the total number of terms in the set. For example, the average of the numbers 1, 2, and 6 is (1 + 2 + 6) / 3, which equals 3. (see **Mean**)

Bar Graph – A graph containing rectangular bars whose lengths correspond to specific amounts of **data**. (see example on page 103)

Base – In a **three-dimensional** object, the **face** around which the object is formed. For example, the base of a triangular **prism** is a **triangle**, and the base of a square **pyramid** is a **square**.

Circle – A circle is formed by using a fixed, imaginary point as a starting point or center, then recording the points around it that are all equal in distance from it. The distance from the center of a circle to its **perimeter** is called the **radius**. The line that travels through the center and divides the circle in half is called the **diameter**; it is equal to twice the length of the radius. The perimeter, or **circumference**, of a circle is found by multiplying the length of the diameter by **pi** (π), which is approximately equal to 3.14 ($C = \pi \times d$). The **area** of a circle is found by multiplying pi by the squared length of the radius ($A = \pi \times r^2$). The number of degrees traveled from a point on a circle back to itself is 360. (see example page 101)

Circle Graph – A type of **graph** usually used to represent **percents**. Its layout is circular, and **data** are given appropriately-sized wedges of the circle based on their corresponding percents. Also called a **pie chart**. (see example on page 103)

Circumference – In a **circle**, the length of the **perimeter** is known as the circle's circumference. The formula for circumference is **pi** times the length of the **diameter** ($C = \pi \times d$).

Commutative Property – For any numbers a and b, in addition: a + b = b + a; in multiplication: a x b = b x a.

Complementary Angles – Two **angles** with a sum of 90°.

Composite Number – A number that has more than two **factors** is called a composite number. Examples include 4, 35, and 121. The numbers zero and one are <u>not</u> composite numbers. (see **Prime Number**)

Cone – A cone is a special type of **pyramid** with a circular base. An example of a cone is an ice cream cone. (see example page 101)

Congruent – Any two figures or measurements which are equal in size or value are referred to as congruent. Congruency applies to the lengths of sides of **polygons** or to **angle** measures. It also applies to polygons as a whole. For example, two **squares** with sides equal in length are said to be congruent to one another. The symbol for congruency is $\cong$. (see **Similar**)

Coordinate – The numerical value, usually expressed in terms of *x* and *y*, of the location of a **point** on a **graph**.

Cross-Multiply – A method used for evaluating whether or not **fractions** are equal. It can be utilized when you have two fractions that are on opposite sides of an equation. For example, if you are asked whether or not 3/4 equals 219/292, you can set them equal to one another and cross multiply: 3/4 = 219/292. To cross-multiply, simply multiply each **numerator** by the **denominator** of the other fraction and drop the original denominator: 3 x 292 = 4 x 219. After evaluating these numbers, you see that: 876 = 876. Yes, these fractions are equal. Cross-multiplication is especially useful when working with **proportions** and **ratios**. For example, if there are 4 oranges for every 5 apples, how many oranges (*n*) are there if there are 95 apples? To solve this, set up an **equation** using the original ratio and the unknown one: 4/5 = n/95. Cross-multiply to get: 380 = 5n. After you divide each side by 5, you find the number of oranges is 76.

Cube – A **three-dimensional** object with 12 **edges** and 6 **faces** that are all **congruent squares**. A cube is a special type of **prism**. The **volume** of a cube is found by multiplying its length times its width times its height (V = l x w x h). An example of a cube is a die. (see example page 101)

Cylinder – A special type of **prism** with a **circle**, instead of a **polygon**, for a **base**. An example of a cylinder is a can. (see example page 101)

Data – A **set** of given information.

Decimal – A decimal is another method of expressing **rational numbers**. Numbers that are **integers** and numbers that are not integers can both be written as decimals. For example, 1 can be written as a decimal in the form 1.0; 1/2 can be written as a decimal in the form 0.5; 3 4/5 can be written as a decimal in the form 3.8. Anything to the right of the decimal point represents a value less than 1. The greater the number to the right of the decimal point, the greater the number is. For example, 0.98 is greater than 0.13; 0.67 is greater than 0.089 (think of this as 0.670 compared to 0.089, or 670 is greater than 89). However, the number 3.1 is greater than 0.9 because the number to the left of the decimal point must always be included when comparing decimals. (see **Place Value**)

Denominator – In a **fraction**, the number below the fraction bar (the "bottom number"). In the case of 1/4, for example, the denominator is 4.

Diameter – In a **circle**, the line which travels through its center from one edge of the circle to the other and divides the circle in half. The length of the diameter is twice the length of the **radius**.

Difference – The **solution** to an **equation** involving subtraction.

Direct Proportion – A method of comparing two equal **ratios**. For example, if for every 3 people there are 2 dogs, how many dogs will there be for 9 people? The direct proportion to solve this sets the original/known ratio of people to dogs equal to the unknown ratio: 3/2 = 9/n or 3/2 = 9/6. In this example, the answer derived from the direct proportion is 6.

Distributive Property – For any numbers a, b, and c: a x (b + c) = a x b + a x c.

Edge – In **three-dimensional** objects, any of the **segments** that define the shape of the **faces** of the object. Edges make up the **perimeter** of each face and the object as a whole. In a **cube**, for example, there are 12 edges.

Equation – Any expression which sets two or more things equal to one another is an equation. An equation can be recognized by the presence of an equal sign (=).

Equiangular – In any given **polygon**, if the measures of all of the **angles** formed by the figure's segments are of equal value (**congruent**), the polygon is said to equiangular. All **regular polygons** are equiangular. Not all polygons that are equiangular are necessarily **equilateral**.

Equilateral – In any given **polygon**, if the lengths of all of the sides are of equal value (**congruent**), the polygon is said to be equilateral. All **regular polygons** are equilateral. All equilateral polygons are **equiangular**. (see example page 101)

Estimate – see **Approximate**; **Rounding**.

Exponent – When a number is raised to a **power**, the power it is raised to is expressed by using an exponent. The exponent shows how many times a number is to be multiplied by itself. An exponent can be any **rational number**, but for the purpose of the FCAT, exponents will only include whole numbers greater than zero. When written, exponents appear after the number they influence and are slightly raised above the number, such as 2^3 or 4^6, where 3 and 6 are the exponents.

Extrapolate – To make a guess based on known information and observation. For example, if you are given the **sequence** of numbers {2, 4, 6, 8,...}, you could predict, based on an observed **pattern**, the next number in the sequence is 10.

Face – In **three-dimensional** objects, the shape that makes up one surface or **side** of the object. For example, in a **cube**, there are 6 faces, all of which are **squares**.

Factor – Any integer you can divide evenly into another number is a factor of that number. The complete **set** of factors for the number 24 is {1, 2, 3, 4, 6, 8, 12, 24}. An important aspect of using factors is being able to find the **prime numbers** that are factors of other numbers. Prime factors break down a number into its most basic parts. Again, use 24 as an example. The prime factors of 24 are 2 x 2 x 2 x 3. This can be seen by taking other factor pairs of 24, such as 4 and 6, and breaking them down into primes: (2 x 2) x (2 x 3). (see **Multiple**)

Flip – When asked to flip an object, students are being asked to move the object around an imaginary **line of symmetry**. The object will maintain its shape, but will be facing a different direction after the flip (mirroring its original position). This is also called a **reflection**. (see example on page 104)

Fraction – A method of expressing **rational numbers**, **ratios**, and division. Fractions are written in the form a/b, where a is the **numerator** and b is the **denominator**. Numbers that are **integers** can be expressed as fractions, such as 3 = 3/1. Rational numbers that are not integers can also be expressed as fractions, such as 0.25 = 1/4. Fractions can be either **proper** or **improper**.

Function – A relation, such as a **graph**, in which a **variable** is dependent on another value. In a graph, each value of x corresponds to a unique value of y.

Graph – A visual method of presenting numerical **data** or **equations**. Some examples of types of graphs are **line graphs**, **pie charts**, **bar graphs**, **scatterplots**, and **pictographs**. (see examples on page 103)

Greatest Common Factor – This is a special type of **factor** between two or more values. It is the highest **integer** which can evenly divide into a **set** of integers. For example, the greatest common factor of 24, 48, and 80 is 8. Even though they also share the factors 2 and 4, 8 is the greatest common factor. The easiest way to determine the greatest common factor is to break the given numbers into their respective **prime** factors, and then take the product of all the terms which are similar. For example, to find the greatest common factor of 81 and 54, simplify them into 3 x 3 x 3 x 3 and 3 x 3 x 3 x 2, respectively. You can see that each number is made up of three 3s, so their greatest common factor is the product of 3 x 3 x 3, or 27. Being able to determine the greatest common factor is especially important for simplifying **fractions**.

Grid – The **intersecting** lines which make up a **graph**. A grid is used to help **plot points**.

Height – For the purposes of geometry, the height is the line drawn from any point on a shape that forms a **perpendicular** line with the side to which it is drawn.

Hexagon – A **polygon** with exactly 6 **sides**. The total measure of the **angles** within a hexagon is 720°. (see example page 101)

Hypotenuse – In a right triangle, the side opposite the right **angle**. It is always the longest side of a right triangle.

Identity Property – For any number a, in addition, a + 0 = 0 + a = a; in multiplication, a x 1 = 1 x a = a.

Improper Fraction – Any fraction in which the **numerator** is greater than or equal to the **denominator** is called an improper fraction. All improper fractions can be converted to **mixed numbers**. By definition, the value of all improper fractions is greater than or equal to one. Examples of improper fractions include 9/5, 26/11, or 100/10.

Inequality – Any expression which denotes two or more things as not equal to one another is an inequality. There are a number of specific inequality types, including less than (<), greater than (>), and not equal to (≠).

Integer – Any number, positive or negative, that is a **whole number** distance away from zero on a number line, in addition to zero. Specifically, an integer is any number in the **set** {...-3, -2, -1, 0, 1, 2, 3...}. Examples of integers include 1, 5, 273, -2, -35, and -1,375.

Intercept – A point on a graph where the line crosses the **y-axis** or **x-axis**. For a linear equation, the intercept occurs when one of the variables is equal to 0.

Intersect – Two lines or **segments** that cross at any given point are said to intersect. Figures, such as **polygons**, are formed by intersecting segments. (see example page 102)

Inverse Property – For any number a, in addition, a – a = 0. In multiplication, for any number $b \neq 0$,

$$b \times \frac{1}{b} = 1.$$

Irrational Numbers – Any **real number** that cannot be expressed as the **ratio** of two **integers** is considered irrational. Some common examples include $\sqrt{2}, \sqrt{3}$, and π.

Isosceles Triangle – A **triangle** with exactly two **sides** of equal length. (see example page 101)

Least Common Denominator – When working with **fractions**, it is often easier to manipulate them when the **denominators** are equal. To find the least common denominator, break the numbers in the denominator into their **prime factors**. Then, multiply each **numerator** and denominator by the factor that is unique to the other denominator. When you multiply the numerator and denominator of a fraction by the same number, it is like multiplying it by one, so you are not really changing the value of the fraction, just its appearance. For example, if you wanted to add 1/4 and 1/6, you would need to find the least common denominator. When you look at the prime factors of the denominators, you find that 4 breaks down into 2 x 2 and 6 breaks down into 3 x 2. Each has at least one 2, so you can ignore those. Because 4 has a unique factor (2), you must multiply the other numerator and denominator (6) by it; and, because 6 has a unique factor (3), you must multiply the other numerator and denominator (4) by it. The fractions become 2/12 and 3/12, respectively. Now that the denominators are equal, adding the two fractions is simply a matter of adding the numerators and maintaining the denominator. In this case, the **solution** is 5/12.

Line Graph – A graph based on an **equation**, such as $3x + 1 = y$ or $x = 3y^2$, which is **plotted** on a **grid** using an **x-axis** and a **y-axis**. The most common example of a line graph is that of the straight line, with an equation $y = mx + b$. In the equation, x and y represent a pair of numbers that make the equation true. This pair of numbers is a **point** on the line. The m is the value of the **slope** of the line, while the b is the value of the equation if x is equal to 0 (this is the y-intercept of the graph, or where the line crosses the **y-axis**). (see example on page 103)

Line of Symmetry – A line, real or imaginary, that divides an object into two **congruent** parts which are mirrored with respect to one another. A **square**, for example, has four lines of symmetry (one vertical; one horizontal; two diagonal). (see example page 102)

Mean – The mean of a **set** of numbers is simply the **average** of the numbers given. For example, in the set {1, 2, 4, 6, 17}, the mean is (1 + 2 + 4 + 6 + 17) / 5, which equals 6. The mean does not have to be a number which appears in the original set. For example, the mean of the set {1, 5, 12} is (1 + 5 + 12) / 3, which equals 6.

Median – In any given **set** of numbers arranged by ascending or descending value, the number which is the exact middle term of the set. For example, in a set of 11 numbers, the sixth term would by the median because it is exactly halfway from the beginning and end of the set. In the set {2, 3, 6, 12, 451}, the median is 6, because it is the third term in the set of 5 numbers. For sets of numbers with an even number of terms, the median is the **average** of the two middle terms. For example, in the set {0, 2, 3, 4, 19, 78}, the median is the average of the third and fourth terms because it is a 6-term set. In this case, the median is 3.5.

Metric System – A **decimal** system of weights and measurements based on the meter and the kilogram. For the purpose of the FCAT, students need not know the relationship between units within the metric system but should be able to identify and use units in proper measurements. The following is a list of the base units of the metric system, as well as a few of their more common derivatives and abbreviations: length – millimeter, centimeter, meter, kilometer (mm, cm, m, km); volume – cubic centimeter, milliliter, liter (cu cm, ml, l); weight – grams, kilograms (g, kg); temperature – degrees Celsius (º C); time – second, minute, hour, day, week, month, year. (see **U.S. System**)

Midpoint – A point on a line **segment** that divides the segment into two **congruent** parts.

Mixed Number – Any **rational number** n where $n < -1$ or $n > 1$ can be expressed as a mixed number, that is in the form of an **integer** and a **proper fraction**. Mixed numbers are often derived from **improper fractions** (all mixed numbers can be written as improper fractions, and vice versa). An example is 7/4, which, when written as a mixed number, is 1 3/4. To convert an improper fraction to a mixed number, first divide the **numerator** by the **denominator**. In the case of 7/4, 4 goes into 7 only once. The number 1 becomes the integer portion of the mixed number. Next, take the remainder from the division and make it the numerator of the proper fraction portion of the mixed number, in this case, 3. Finally, use the denominator of the improper fraction, which is 4, as the denominator of the proper fraction. By doing this, we see 7/4 is the same as 1 3/4. An easy way to tell whether or not an improper fraction equals a mixed number is to find the decimal value of each; they should be equal.

Mode – In any given **set** of numbers, the mode is the number that occurs most often. For example, in the set {1, 2, 2, 3, 3, 4, 4, 4}, the mode is 4. If more than one number occurs the greatest number of times, then there are multiple modes. For example, in the set {1, 1, 2, 2, 3}, the modes are 1 and 2. If every number in a set occurs the same number of times, there is no mode. Unlike **mean** and **median**, the mode of a set is always a number that occurs somewhere in the set.

Multiple – Any number which is the product of two integers is said to be a multiple of those numbers. For example, some multiples of the number 4 are 8, 12, 36, and 4,000, which are (4 x 2), (4 x 3), (4 x 9), and (4 x 1,000), respectively. In each case, the number is a multiple of 4, while individually, the products are multiples of both 4 and 2, 4 and 3, 4 and 9, and 4 and 1,000, respectively. (see **Factor**)

Natural Numbers – The **set** of **integers** used for counting, {1, 2, 3, 4, 5 . . .}.

Numerator – In a **fraction,** the number which appears above the fraction bar (the "top number"). In the fraction 5/8, for example, the numerator is 5.

Obtuse – An **angle** with a measure between 90º and 180º. (see example page 102)

Octagon – A **polygon** with exactly 8 sides. The total measure of the **angles** within an octagon is 1080º. (see example page 101)

Order of Operations – When solving any **equation**, there is a proper order of operations to consider: parentheses, **exponents**, multiplication, division, addition, subtraction. An easy way to remember this is by using the mnemonic device "please excuse my dear Aunt Sally," or PEMDAS. For an example of the proper order of operations, consider the following: $(40 + 40) \div 2 - 2^2 \times 3$. Students would first do the math inside the parentheses, resulting in $80 / 2 - 2^2 \times 3$. Next, students would raise the 2 by a **power** of 2: $80 \div 2 - 4 \times 3$. Multiplication is next: $80 \div 2 - 12$. Then division, $40 - 12$. Finally, because there is no addition left to do, subtract; the result is 28.

Ordered Pair – see **Point**.

Origin – A special **coordinate** on a **line graph** with value (0, 0). It is not in any specific **quadrant**. (see example page 103)

Parallel – When two lines, **segments**, or rays travel in such a way that they will never **intersect** if continued, they are said to be parallel to one another. The **symbol** denoting parallel lines is ||. (see example page 102)

Parallelogram – A **quadrilateral** with both pairs of opposite sides **parallel** to one another. Each side is equal in length to the side opposite it. The **area** of a parallelogram is found by multiplying the length of the base by the length of the height ($A = b \times h$). Special cases of parallelograms include **rectangles** and **rhombi**. (see example page 101)

Pattern – A repeatable occurrence in a given **set** or **sequence** of numbers or figures. In the sequence {1, 2, 3, 4, 5...}, for example, the pattern is to add 1 to the number to obtain the next number in the sequence. A pattern is sometimes referred to as a **trend**.

Pentagon – A **polygon** with exactly 5 sides. The total measure of the **angles** within a pentagon is 540°. (see example page 101)

Percent – When you take a specific part of a value, this is referred to as taking a percent of the original value. Percent literally means "per hundred" and is represented by the **symbol** %. Any given percent can be written fractionally as that number over a **denominator** of 100 (all percents can be expressed as **fractions**, and vice versa). For example, the expression 25% can be thought of fractionally as 25/100 or 1/4. Percents are useful because they can be used as **direct proportions**. For example, if you want to know what 75% of 576 is, set up the following proportion: $75 / 100 = n / 576$. You could also evaluate this by changing 75% into its equivalent fraction, 3/4, and multiplying by 576: $3/4 \times 576$. Percents are also used to represent **probability**.

Perimeter – The total length of the outside border of an object is called its perimeter. For any **polygon**, the actual value is determined by finding the sum of the lengths of all of its sides. For example, a triangle with sides of 5 inches, 4 inches, and 3 inches has a perimeter of 12 inches. The **units of measurement** used to express perimeter are linear units, such as inches or kilometers. The most common abbreviation for perimeter is P.

Perpendicular – When two lines, **segments**, or rays **intersect** and form **right angles**, they are said to be perpendicular to one another. The **symbol** for perpendicular is ⊥. (see example page 102)

Pi – A number that expresses the **ratio** of the **circumference** of a **circle** to its **diameter**. It is represented by the **symbol** π and is used in circles to find both **area** and circumference. Pi is approximately equal to 3.14 or 22/7.

Pictograph – A graph that represents **data** using pictures rather than lines or numbers. A pictograph always has a corresponding key to tell what information the picture represents. (see example on page 103)

Pie Chart – see **Circle Graph**.

Place Value – The location of a specific digit in any given number. Consider the following number for a description of specific place values: 1,234,567.890. The 1 is in the millions place; the 2 is in the hundred thousands place; the 3 is in the ten thousands place; the 4 is in the thousands place; the 5 is in the hundreds place; the 6 is in the tens place; the 7 is in the ones place; the 8 is in the tenths place; the 9 is in the hundredths place; and the 0 is in the thousandths place.

Place value is essential when comparing the size of numbers. When comparing numbers, first look at the leftmost digit of each number. The number with a digit in the leftmost place value is greater. If both numbers have digits in that place value, the number with the greater digit in that place value is greater.

Plane – Any region which can be defined by a minimum of three **points** common only to that region. A plane is a region that extends infinitely in a **two-dimensional** manner.

Plot – To place **points** at their proper **coordinates** on a **graph**.

Point – A location on a **graph** defined by its position in relation to the **x-axis** and **y-axis**. Points are sometimes called **ordered pairs** and are written in this form: (x-**coordinate**, y-coordinate).

Polygon – A closed **two-dimensional** figure of three or more sides formed by segments that meet only at their endpoints; no more than two segments meet at any given endpoint. Examples of polygons include **triangles**, **rectangles**, **parallelograms**, **pentagons**, **hexagons**, and **octagons**. A general formula to find the sum of **angles** for any polygon is to subtract 2 from the number of sides, then multiply this number by 180° (sum of angles = $(n - 2)$ x 180°). Special polygons that have sides of equal length are called **regular polygons**. (For examples, see page 101)

Power – When a number is raised by an **exponent**, it is said to be raised by that power. For example, 3^4 can be thought of as the fourth power of three. To find the actual value, multiply the base number, in this case 3, by itself the number of times equal to the value of the exponent, in this case 4, which equates to 3 x 3 x 3 x 3. Therefore, the fourth power of three equals 81.

Prime Number – A number that is not evenly divisible by any number other than itself and the number one is referred to as prime. Prime numbers are the **factors** of **composite numbers** (numbers that are not prime). Examples of prime numbers include 13, 23, and 61. The numbers zero and one are **not** prime numbers; the only even prime number is 2. Prime numbers cannot be negative.

Prism – A **three-dimensional** object formed by connecting the corresponding **vertexes** of two **congruent, parallel faces** that are **polygons**. The **volume** of any prism is found by multiplying its length times its width times its height (V = l x w x h). (see example page 101)

Probability – The likelihood that an event will occur. Specifically, probability is the number of desired events divided by the number of possible outcomes. For example, when finding the probability of flipping a coin and having it land on heads, the number of desired events equals 1, and the number of possible outcomes equals 2. Probability is most often recorded in **ratios** or **percents**; therefore, in the example, the probability of flipping a coin and having it land on heads is 1:2 or 1/2 or 50%.

Product – The **solution** to an **equation** involving multiplication.

Proper Fraction – Any fraction with the **numerator** less than the **denominator** is called a proper fraction. By definition, the value of all proper fractions is less than one. Examples of proper fractions include 1/2, 5/16, 786/5563, and 2/17.

Properties – Known interactions of numbers in specific situations in addition and multiplication. (see **Associative Property, Commutative Property, Distributive Property, Identity Property, Inverse Property** and **Zero Property**)

Proportion – see **Direct Proportion**.

Pyramid – A **three-dimensional** figure with a **polygon** for a base, with the rest of the **faces** formed by connecting **segments** from each **vertex** of the polygon to a common vertex away from the base. (see example page 101)

Pythagorean Theorem – In any **right triangle**, the **sum** of the squares of the lengths of the two sides **perpendicular** to one another is equal to the square of the length of the **hypotenuse**: $a^2 + b^2 = c^2$.

Quadrant – Any one of four unique sections of a **two-dimensional graph**. Quadrant I contains the points for which x and y are both positive; Quadrant II contains the points for which x is negative and y is positive; Quadrant III contains the points for which x and y are both negative; and Quadrant IV contains the points for which x is positive and y is negative. (see example page 103)

Quadrilateral – Any **polygon** with exactly four sides is called a quadrilateral. Some types of quadrilaterals have special names and properties, including **rectangles, squares, parallelograms, rhombi,** and **trapezoids**.

Quotient – The **solution** to an **equation** involving division.

Radical – A mathematical operation symbolized by $\sqrt{\ }$. A radical is any number or expression which has a root. (see **Square Root**)

Radius – The length from the center of a **circle** to its **perimeter**. The value of the radius is equal to half the length of the **diameter**.

Range – In a **set** of numbers, the difference between the two extremes in the set; in other words, the maximum value in a set minus the minimum value in a set. For example, the range of the set {2, 5, 8, 23, 46} is 46 – 2 = 44.

Rate – A rate is an expression of how long it takes to do something. Examples of rates are miles per hour and revolutions per minute. In general, rate is measured as an event divided by a unit of time.

Ratio – A ratio is a comparison of two numbers. Ratios can be expressed in one of the following ways: 3/1 or 3:1 or 3 to 1. In this example, all of the ratios are equal. Ratios can be used to compare like and different items. For example, a ratio may indicate that for every 3 apples grown, 1 was eaten; or it may show that for every 3 apples grown, 1 orange was also grown. Ratios are also used to express **direct proportions** and **probability**.

Rational Number – A number that can be formed as the **ratio** of two **integers**. Examples include 2 (written as a ratio: 2/1), .5 (written as a ratio: 1/2), and 1.75 (written as a ratio: 7/4).

Ray – A line that travels infinitely in one direction from a given point.

Real Number – Any number that is either **rational** or **irrational** is in the **set** of real numbers. Real numbers are any values you might come across in real life. Examples of real numbers include -2, 0, 0.15, 1/2, $\sqrt{3}$, π, and 7.89 x 10^9.

Rectangle – A **quadrilateral** with each pair of opposite sides parallel to one another and whose sides meet at **right angles**. A rectangle is a special type of **parallelogram**. A **square** is a special type of rectangle. The **area** of a rectangle is found by multiplying its length by its width (A = l x w). (see example page 101)

Reduce – To put a **fraction** into its simplest form by dividing out any common factors. For example, 4/8 reduces to 1/2 in its simplest form.

Reflection – see **Flip**.

Regular polygons – A special type of **polygon** that is both **equilateral** and **equiangular**.

Rhombus – A rhombus is a **quadrilateral,** and more specifically, a special type of **parallelogram** having four sides of equal length with each pair of opposite sides **parallel** to each other. The **area** of a rhombus is found by multiplying the length of the base by the length of the height (A = b x h). A special type of rhombus is a **square**. (see example page 101)

Right Angle – An **angle** with a measure of exactly 90°. The lines or **segments** which form right angles are said to be **perpendicular** to one another. (see example page 102)

Rotation – When asked to rotate an object, students are being asked to move the object around an imaginary point in a circular motion. After the move, the object will have the same shape and size but will be facing a different direction. This is also known as a **turn**. (see example on page 104)

Rounding – Taking an exact value and making it an **approximation**. Rounding is done by examining the value of the number in the **place value** to the right of the place value to which you want to round. If this number is less than 5 in value, you round down; if it is equal to 5 or greater, you round up. To round the number 114 to the nearest ten, you first examine the number in the ones place because it is to the right of the tens place. Because this number is less than 5, you round down to the nearest ten. To do this, look at the numbers that make up the places up to and including the place you want to round to, in this case, the tens place. The number is 14, so you round down to the nearest ten, which is 10. The value of 114 rounded to the nearest ten is therefore 110. For another example, round 368 to the nearest ten. Since the ones place is occupied by a number greater than 5, you round up in this situation. The nearest ten up from this number is 370. Finally, round the number 10.35 to the nearest tenth. Because the number to the right of the tenths place is equal to 5, you must round up. The nearest tenth rounded up, in this situation, is 10.4. Rounding can be done for numbers in any place value.

Ruler – A straight-edged instrument used for measuring the lengths of objects. A ruler usually has inches or centimeters for its units.

Scatterplot – A type of **graph** containing **points** similar to those found on a line graph, except the points are not contained within one specific **equation**. This type of graph is usually used when data seems more random than ordered. (see example on page 103)

Scientific Notation – A method of writing any **rational number** in **decimal** form multiplied by a **power** of ten. When expressing numbers in scientific notation, there are two parts to the expression: the decimal number and the power of ten by which it is multiplied. Scientific notation is most often used with numbers that are very small or very large. To express a number in scientific notation, the number must first be written in decimal form. Once this is done, move the decimal point between the first two non-zero digits. For large numbers greater than one, move the decimal point to the left; for small numbers less than one, the decimal point moves to the right. Now that the decimal point has been moved, you must account for the **place values** you have lost. This is where the power of ten comes in. Count the number of places the decimal point moved; this number is the power by which ten should be raised in the scientific notation. When you move the decimal point to the left, the power is positive; when you move the decimal point to the right, the power is negative.

To express the number 1,976 in scientific notation, move the decimal point so it is located between the first two non-zero numbers, in this case 1 and 9: 1.976. Note, usually the first step is converting numbers into decimal form, but 1,976 is in decimal form already (think of it as 1,976.0). Now, count the number of places the decimal point was moved. In this case it moved three places to the left. You can now express 1,976 in scientific notation: 1.976×10^3. To check to see if this is the same number you started with, think of it as 1.976×1000 (which is 10^3). You can see that this equals 1,976.

To express 627/10,000 in scientific notation, first convert the fraction to a decimal, which is .0627. Next, move the decimal point between the first two non-zero digits, in this case 6 and 2: 6.27. Now, count the number of places to the right the decimal point was moved, and you find it is two. Because you moved the decimal point to the right, the power of ten is the negative value of this number, so the scientific notation of 627/10,000 is 6.27×10^{-2}.

Segment – A line ending at specific points. Segments meet at vertexes to form closed figures, both two- and three-dimensional.

Semicircle – Half of a **circle** with the **diameter** as its base.

Sequence – Any ordered **set** of numbers or objects produced by an observable **pattern** is called a sequence. Perhaps the most basic sequence of numbers is the numbers used when counting: 1, 2, 3, 4, 5, ... A definite pattern can be seen, and we can predict how the sequence will continue. Another example of a numerical sequence is: 1, 1, 1, 1, 1, 1, ... Although the numbers in the set never change, we can observe this as a pattern and thus determine that the sequence will continue in a similar fashion. Sequences can also include geometric shapes. For example, if you see a **triangle** followed by a **square** followed by a triangle followed by a square, you can safely assume that this is a sequence, which will continue with a triangle.

Set – Any grouping of numbers. A set can be specific or random, small or large. Sets are usually notated by placing numbers within brackets, as with {1, 2, 3}. Before finding statistical **data** of sets, you should always arrange the values in descending or ascending order.

Side – In any **polygon**, a segment which is part of its construction. The number of sides helps define what specific type of polygon a figure is. Some examples include **triangles**, which have 3 sides; **quadrilaterals**, which have 4 sides; and **pentagons**, which have 5 sides. In **three-dimensional** figures, the word side is often used to refer to the **face** of the object.

Similar – Two **polygons** are said to be similar to one another if they have an equal number of sides with corresponding **angles** of equal measure. For example, all **squares** are similar to each other, but not necessarily **congruent**, because by definition all squares have four **right angles**. Figures whose definitions do not rely on angle measure are not necessarily similar. For example, although **triangles** can be similar or congruent, they do not have to be because the measures of their angles can vary (an **equilateral** triangle is neither congruent nor similar to a **right triangle**).

Slide – When asked to slide an object, students are being asked to move it a certain distance while maintaining the size and orientation (direction) of the object. This is also known as **translation**. (see example on page 104)

Slope – The amount of change in the y-**coordinate** with respect to the amount of change in the x-coordinate in a straight line on a **graph**. It is represented by the constant m in the equation $y = mx + b$. Slope can be found by taking any two **points** on a line, finding the difference in the x values, and then dividing that difference by the difference in the corresponding y values. For example, if two points on a line were (3, 2) and (1, 0), the slope of that line would be $(3 – 1) / (2 – 0) = 2 / 2 = 1$. Slope can also be negative, as seen in a line with points (2, 5) and (4, 1): $(2 – 4) / (5 – 1) = -2 / 4 = -1/2$. You will be able to tell whether the slope of a line is positive or negative by looking at the graph. The slope will be positive if the line rises from left to right; it will be negative if the slope descends from left to right.

Solution – The answer to an **equation** that is being solved.

Solve – A term used when evaluating **equations**, **variables**, and **unknowns**. To solve the equation $3 + 3 = n$, the value of the unknown n is the **solution**, which in this case is 6. The solution of an equation containing variables is dependent on the value of one of the variables. For example, if given the equation $n – 1 = y$, students may be asked to solve for y if $n = 2$. In this case, the solution is 1.

Sphere – A **three-dimensional** object formed by taking a **radius** of given length and revolving it three-dimensionally around a given point. The shape formed represents any area that the radius may possibly travel through. An example of a sphere is a baseball. (see example page 101)

Square – A **quadrilateral** with each pair of opposite sides **parallel** to each other, all sides equal in length, and sides that meet at **right angles**. By definition, a square is also a **rectangle**, a **parallelogram**, and a **rhombus**. The **area** of a square is found by multiplying its length by its width (A = l x w). (see example page 101)

Square Root – When a number is multiplied by itself, it is said to be the square root of the resulting **product**. For example, because 5 x 5 = 25, 5 is the square root of 25. The **symbol** for square root is a **radical** sign.

Straight Angle – An angle with a measure of 180°; this is a straight line.

Sum – The **solution** to an **equation** involving addition.

Supplementary Angle – Two **angles** with a sum of 180°.

Symbol – A symbol is a method of representing a number, an **unknown** value, and/or a word or words by using other characters. Symbols can be letters, as they often are for unknowns and **variables**, and they can also be specialized characters, such as $, which means dollars, or >, which means greater than. Symbols can also be used to represent mathematical actions or procedures. For example, in this book, multiplication is represented by this symbol: x.

Symmetric – An object is said to exhibit symmetry if it is possible to split the object with any line, real or imaginary (see **Line of Symmetry**), and produce two new objects with identical attributes. For example, in a **circle**, the **diameter** divides the circle into two equal **semicircles**. These semicircles are symmetric because they are equal in relation to the diameter. If you divide a **square** in half, it also exhibits symmetry. However, in a **rectangle**, for example, symmetry is only exhibited when the lines are drawn horizontally or vertically through the center of the rectangle. Although drawing a line diagonally through the center produces two equal (**congruent**) halves, they are not symmetrical around the line. A good way to picture symmetry is to draw a line through an object and mentally fold the object on that line. If the two halves match up exactly, the figure is symmetrical.

Tessellation – A pattern formed by placing congruent figures together with no empty space or overlapping areas. An example of a tessellation is a checkerboard.

Three-Dimensional – Having measurable properties of length, width, and height. (see figures on page 101)

Translation – see **Slide**.

Trapezoid – A special type of **quadrilateral** with only one pair of opposite **sides parallel** to each other. The **area** of a trapezoid is found by multiplying the **sum** of its parallel sides by its height, then dividing by two (A = [h x (sum of parallel sides) / 2]). (see example page 101)

Tree Diagram – A visual diagram of all the possible outcomes for a certain event. A tree diagram is used to show the **probability** of a certain event happening. The example on page 103 shows a tree diagram for flipping a coin three times. (see example page 103)

Trend – A noticeable, repeatable **pattern** that is not necessarily exact. Trends can be used to make **approximations** about **unknown** values, such as future events or measurements. (see **Pattern**)

Triangle – Any **polygon** having exactly three sides is called a triangle. The sum of the **angles** of a triangle is always equal to 180°. To find the area of any triangle, multiply the length of the base by its height and then divide by 2: (A = b x h / 2). Some special types of triangles include **equilateral**, **isosceles**, and **right triangles**. (see example page 101)

Turn – see **Rotation**.

Two-Dimensional – Having measurable properties of length and width only. (see figures on page 101)

U.S. System of Measurement – This is the system of measurement which most people in the United States still use; the rest of the world, for the most part, uses the **metric system**. The following is a list of common U.S. units of measurement along with their abbreviations: length – inches, feet, yards, miles (in., ft., yd., mi.,); volume – fluid ounces, teaspoons, tablespoons, cups, pints, quarts, gallons (fl. oz., tsp., tbsp., pt., qt., gal.); weight – ounces, pounds, tons (oz., lb., t.); temperature – degrees Fahrenheit (° F); time – second, minute, hour, day, week, month, year. Also called customary units.

Units of Measurement – Units of measurement are used to record how specific values relate to the objects from which they were taken. Units not only give clues as to what type of measurement is being made, but also relate to the size of the measurement. For example, if a measurement is recorded as 5 inches, you know the measurement is an object's length. If a measurement is 1 mile, even though the number is small, you know this is a relatively large distance.

When recording units of measurement, there are two common systems that are utilized: the **U.S. system** and the **metric system**. Each system has its own units which students must be able to recognize and use. Common attributes which are measured include length, volume, weight, speed, temperature, and time. Although it is not necessary for students to memorize the conversions from one system to the other, they should be able to recognize units of similar size. For example, pounds would be used in the same situation as kilograms, but grams would most likely not be used; for grams, a similar unit might be ounces. Students should also be able to identify units of measurement based on common abbreviations, such as in. for inches or m for meters.

A conversion table is provided for you below to use with the chapter questions and practice assessment test at the end of the chapter.

Conversions:

1 yard = 3 feet = 36 inches
1 mile = 1,760 yards = 5,280 feet
1 acre = 43,560 square feet
1 hour = 60 minutes; 1 minute = 60 seconds
1 pound = 16 ounces
1 ton = 2,000 pounds
1 cup = 8 fluid ounces; 1 pint = 2 cups; 1 quart = 2 pints; 1 gallon = 4 quarts

1 liter = 1000 milliliters = 1000 cubic centimeters
1 meter = 100 centimeters = 1000 millimeters; 1 kilometer = 1000 meters
1 gram = 1000 milligrams; 1 kilogram = 1000 grams

Unknown – The part of an **equation** which is not known and must be solved for. Unknowns can be represented by letters or other **symbols**. For example, in the equation $2n = 6$, the unknown is represented by the letter n. The value of the unknown, in this case, is 3.

Variable – In an **equation**, a value which can change and affect the overall value of the expression. Variables are represented by letters such as n or y. For example, in the equation $3n + 1 = y$, the value of y will vary as the value of n changes, and vice versa. If $n = 1$, then $y = 4$, but if $n = 3$, $y = 10$. Variables are a special type of **unknown** that are always dependent on other information.

Vertex – In a **two-dimensional** object, any point where two **segments** join to form an angle. In a **three-dimensional** object, any point where three or more segments join to form a corner of the object. In a **cube**, for example, there are 8 vertices.

Vertical Angles – The pair of **angles** opposite to one another at the point where two lines, **segments**, or **rays intersect**. Vertical angles are always **congruent** to one another.

Volume – The amount of area taken up by a **three-dimensional** object is known as its volume. In its simplest expression, volume is an object's length multiplied by its width multiplied by its height/depth. The **units of measurement** used to express volume can be cubic units, such as cubic feet or cubic centimeters, or, when measuring fluids, units such as gallons or liters. Volume is usually abbreviated as V and is also called capacity.

Whole Number – An **integer** in the **set** {0, 1, 2, 3…}. In other words, a whole number is any number used when counting, in addition to zero.

X-axis – On a **graph**, the number line which runs horizontally. (see example on page 103)

Y-axis – On a **graph**, the number line which runs vertically. (see example on page 103)

Zero Property – For any number a, in addition: a + 0 = a; in multiplication: a x 0 = 0.

Examples of Common Two-Dimensional Shapes

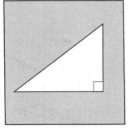

Right Triangle

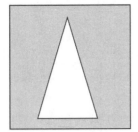

Isosceles Triangle

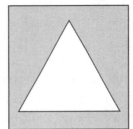

Equilateral Triangle

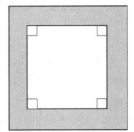

Square

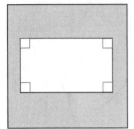

Rectangle

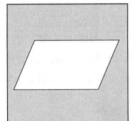

Parallelogram

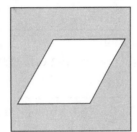

Rhombus

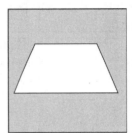

Trapezoid

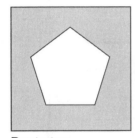

Pentagon

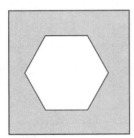

Hexagon

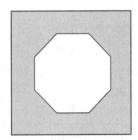

Octagon

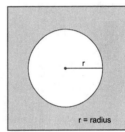

r = radius

Circle

Examples of Common Three-Dimensional Shapes

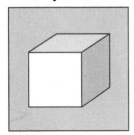

Cube

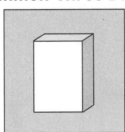

Rectangular Prism

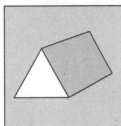

Triangular Prism

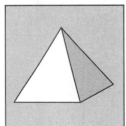

Pyramid

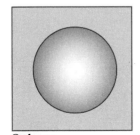

Sphere

Cylinder

Cone

Examples of How Lines Interact

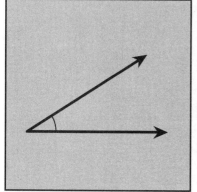

Acute Angle

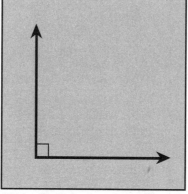

Right Angle

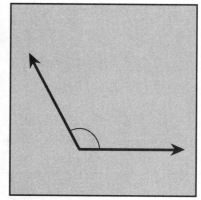

Obtuse Angle

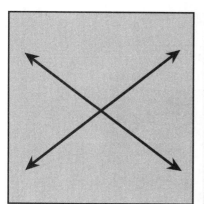

Intersecting Lines

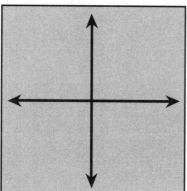

Perpendicular Lines

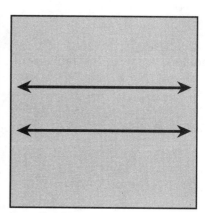

Parallel Lines

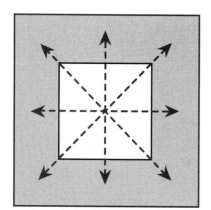

Lines of Symmetry

Examples of Types of Graphs

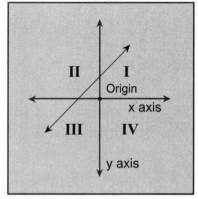

Line Graph

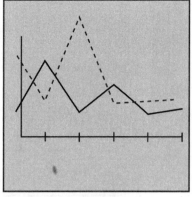

Double Line Graph

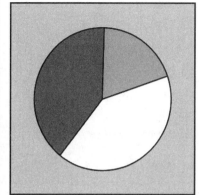

Pie Chart

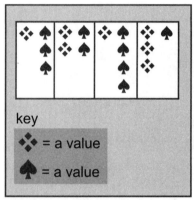

Pictograph

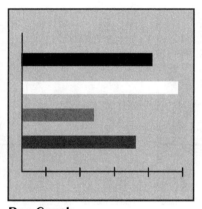

Bar Graph

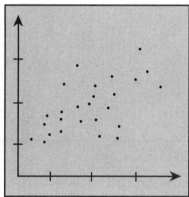

Scatterplot

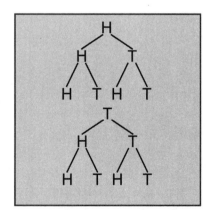

Tree Diagram

Examples of Object Movement

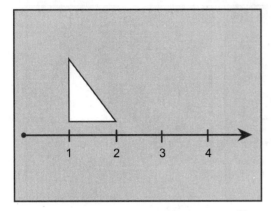 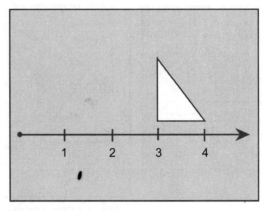

Translation

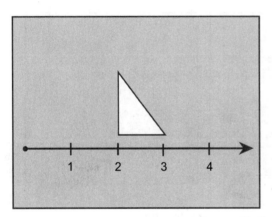 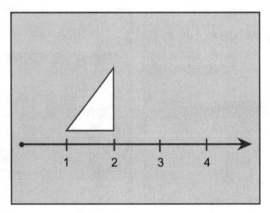

Reflection

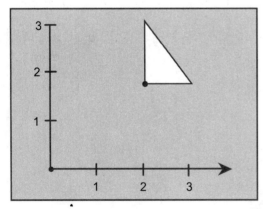 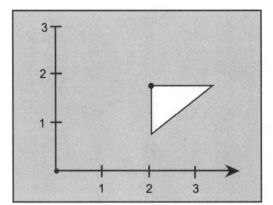

Rotation

Commonly Used Equations

Linear Equations:

Formula for a line: $y = mx + b$

Slope of a line: $m = \dfrac{y_2 - y_1}{x_2 - x_1}$

Distance between two points on a line: $d = \sqrt{(x_1 - x_2)^2 + (y_1 - y_2)^2}$

Midpoint between two points on a line: $M = [\,\dfrac{(x_1 + x_2)}{2}, \dfrac{(y_1 + y_2)}{2}\,]$

Geometric Equations:

Two-dimensional objects:

Circle: Circumference $= d \times \pi$
    Area $= \pi \times r^2$

Triangle: Area $= \dfrac{b \times h}{2}$

Square and Rectangle: Area $= l \times w$

Parallelogram and Rhombus: Area $= b \times h$

Trapezoid: Area $= \dfrac{h \times (b_1 + b_2)}{2}$

Sum of interior angles $= (n - 2) \times 180°$

Three-dimensional objects:

Sphere: Volume $= \dfrac{4 \times \pi \times r^3}{3}$

Cube and Rectangular Prism: Volume $= l \times w \times h$

Cylinder: Volume $= \pi \times h \times r^2$

Cone: Volume $= \dfrac{\pi \times h \times r^2}{3}$

General Prism: Volume $=$ Area of the base $\times h$

General Pyramid: Volume $= \dfrac{\text{Area of the base} \times h}{3}$

Other Equations:

Pythagorean Theorem: $a^2 + b^2 = c^2$; a = side, b = side, c = hypotenuse

Formula for Distance: $D = r \times t$; r = rate, t = time

Pi: $\pi = 3.14$ or $\dfrac{22}{7}$

Thank YOU
For Your Purchase!

For more information on FCAT products,

call 1-877-PASSING (727-7464), or

visit our website:

www.showwhatyouknowpublishing.com